THE MODERN NOVEL

SOME ASPECTS OF
CONTEMPORARY FICTION

THE MODERN NOVEL

SOME ASPECTS OF
CONTEMPORARY FICTION

By

ELIZABETH A. DREW, 1887-1965

KENNIKAT PRESS, INC./PORT WASHINGTON, N.Y.

PR
881
. D7
1967

To
MY MOTHER

Contents

Introduction

> There are two things that I am confident I can do very well. One is an introduction to any literary work, stating what it is to contain, and how it should be executed in the most perfect manner. The other is a conclusion, shewing from various causes why the execution has not been equal to what the author promised to himself and to the publick.
> —DR. JOHNSON

MR. J. B. CABELL declares in one of his essays that intelligent persons do not attempt to keep abreast of modern fiction, and that this is probably ascribable to the fact that they enjoy being intelligent and wish to remain so. This seems a little harsh. The novel is the most popular literary form of the present day, and any one who is not interested in the literature which is produced by his own day can hardly be very intelligently interested in literature. Again, intelligent persons are usually curious as to the human, social, moral and intellectual conundrums and conditions in whose midst they live, and at no time have the stir of such problems been so much the matter of literature as they are in the modern novel. It reflects, more than any other form of writing, the social consciousness of the modern world. Readers may not approve of modern fiction. They may dislike sex novels, or psychology, or prose that breaks out into a rash of spotty adjectives and images. They may venerate the Victorians and want to cry "Avenge, O Lord, thy slaughtered saints whose bones" have been so bleached by the cold touch of superior modern irony, but whether they are in agreement or disagreement with the conclusions and methods of either Victorians or moderns, they can equally be interested to mark and comment on their differences. No age is the Law and the Prophets. We are eternally sowing our future and reaping our past, and as we thus cultivate our collective garden, most of us have some feeling of inquisitiveness about the quality of the rotating crops.

There are, of course, readers who only use novels as a kind of drug: the type of reader incarnated into that semi-mythological figure, the Tired Business Man, and the sort of fiction created for that public needs no discussion. To criticize some of it would be, as Dr. Johnson said of criticizing the absurdities of the last act of *Cymbeline*, to waste comment on "unresisting imbecility," for more often than not writer and reader might be summed up as two minds without a single thought. But even the best of that type need no examination. We all have moods when we respond wholeheartedly to a good detective story or a P. G. Wodehouse comedy, but they are not moods of literary and social criticism.

There is plenty of room, however, for the discussion of the serious novel of to-day. Even if one does not conform to that definition of an optimist as some one who believes what is said on the paper jacket of a new book, it is nevertheless impossible to be unconscious of the very large amount of extremely competent novel writing of the present, and of its significance in the life of the time. For the intelligent reader who doesn't just read to kill time—who prefers time alive, not dead—the reader who doesn't just want a book to read, but prefers to *read* a *book*, there is certainly no lack of material in modern fiction. These essays attempt a review of such material. They aim at a discussion of what is most lively and characteristic in the manners and morals of our age, and their treatment in our most lively and characteristic literary form. The book cannot pretend to be an adequate survey of the whole of contemporary English and American fiction. It only mentions such novels as the writer happens to have read, and to have considered the best and the most significant to illustrate the various topics examined. Needless to say, neither can it pretend to be dispassionate. Papini wrote in one of his prefaces, "There is not an impersonal page in this book; these essays are all partial and subjective," and Anatole France declares: "When I say I am going to talk about Shakespeare and Racine, I mean that I am going to talk about myself in relation to Shakespeare and Racine." That is what we all mean when we set out to discuss. The novel, and especially the contemporary novel, is a subject on which everybody holds definite and determined views, and no single critic can possibly expect complete agreement from his readers. It would indeed be very dull if he got it: for surely criticism does not spring from any obscure inner necessity to make solemn laws for literature or for life, but rather from a sociable and urbane liking to provoke "great argument about it and about."

The Plain Reader

The Plain Reader

If all the good people were clever
And all clever people were good,
The world would be better than ever
We thought that it possibly could;

But somehow 'tis seldom or never
The two hit it off as they should,
The good are so harsh to the clever
The clever so rude to the good.
—Elizabeth Wordsworth

And the rudeness of the clever to the good is expressed nowhere more caustically than when the aesthetes address the general public on the subject of literary appreciation. "Any one who has anything to say cannot fail to be misunderstood," says Mr. Cardan in *Those Barren Leaves*. "The public only understands the things with which it is perfectly familiar. Something new makes it lose its orientation." Or we can hear Mr. Mencken cackling triumphantly as he scores hit upon palpable hit on the subject of the Nordic incapacity to comprehend art and the artist. It is all quite true. The vast majority of the public are in the position of Florence in *The Constant Nymph* as she argues with her artist husband.

3

"You put the wrong things first. Music, all art—
What is it for? What is its justification? After all . . ."

"It's not for anything. It has no justification."

"It's only part of the supreme art, the business of living
beautifully. You can't put it on a pedestal above decency
and humanity and civilization. . . ."

"I know. You want to use it like electric light. . . . I've
seen it: my father's cultured—"

"That is a much abused word, but it means an important
thing which we can't do without."

"Can't we? I can! By God, I can!"

The pure artist claims, as Lewis Dodd claims here, to
be creator and nothing else, and demands to be judged
as such. Literature, however, with the possible exception of what Mr. George Moore calls pure poetry, differs
from the other major arts by its far closer approach to
the terms of actual life. In a sense this makes it easier
for the general public to appreciate, but in another
sense it complicates the outlook. It has led to the un-
ending strife among the critics as to the plane on which
enjoyment of literature should function, and the poor
reading public, sincerely anxious to know what books
to read, and what to look for in the books it reads,
finds itself confused and fuddled by the contradictory
advices of the experts. It knows, from the rude things
which the superior intellectuals say about it, that its
natural instinct to regard literary values exactly as if
they were moral values, and to judge books as it would
human conduct, is inadequate and misleading; but how
is it to choose an alternative? It reads books in a

straightforward way, and wants to criticize them in a straightforward way, but there are the Art for Art's sakers who demand a purely aesthetic standard, making of literature, as of the fine arts, an exclusive cult for exclusive people. The intellectual theorists are not very much more helpful, even though Matthew Arnold and Pater, the literary philosophers, with their somewhat vague talk of abstractions like Beauty and Good and Sweetness and Light and hard gemlike flames of the mind, have been followed by the newer race of literary psychologists; then there are the social historians like Taine, generalizing all individuality into a national and historical significance, with the anatomists to whom technique means everything, and finally the mere gossips who deal in nothing but the froth of personalities.

It is no wonder if the patient dies while all these doctors disagree, yet the holding of some standard of appreciation is essential to the intelligent enjoyment of reading, even of novel reading. The novel may be an amusement for an idle hour, but it may equally be, as Jane Austen claims for it, "a work in which the greatest powers of the mind are displayed: in which the most thorough knowledge of human nature, the happiest delineations of its varieties, the liveliest effusions of wit and humour, are conveyed to the world in the best chosen language." It is worth considering, therefore, how a novel which is a serious work of literature should be approached, for it is an inquiry which is of importance to all readers and to all writers of novels, that is, to a majority of the inhabitants of the English-speaking world.

It may, I think, be of some help, if, before arguing further about literary appreciation, we go back another step, to the root of the matter, and ask the basic question what literature *is*. Sir Arthur Quiller-Couch has defined it, "what sundry men and women have said memorably concerning life," which is, perhaps, as good a working definition as it is possible to find. As modern scholarship enables us to see further and further into past civilizations and "the dark backward and abyss of time," the more apparent does it become that human nature remains unchanged. Egyptian, Greek, Chinese, Hindu, medieval, Renaissance or modern European thinkers and creators, tell the same stories, and distil the same comments from them as to the nature of life and of mankind. Men and women all down the ages have faced the same eternal human problems and have asked the same eternal human questions as they found themselves confronted by the same harsh interplay of human venture and event, the same clash of opposites which forever thwart and jar each other in human existence: aspiration and achievement, physical and spiritual, actual and ideal, good and evil, life and death. Meanwhile, all those who have had what we vaguely call the gift of expression, have always striven to describe in words something of what they have seen, something of what they have heard, something of what they have thought, something of what they have felt, in this eternal and unchanging drama, the author of the Book of Job crying with the same voice as Oedipus or Milton's Samson, "God of our Fathers, what is Man?" No writer can ever solve the riddle: the characters he creates are but comments suggested by his own mind, the stories he tells are but illustrations evolved by his own mind, and these comments and illustrations vary with every age and nationality and individual. But the aim of each in turn is always and eternally the same: to give some created vision of what life is, it may be to fall into the baffling fascination of attempting to explain its why; and the unfading interest for the reader is to compare epochs and peoples and personalities as they practise this single aim: to watch each one, from Confucius to Conrad, from Sophocles to Shaw, as he illustrates and interprets human existence in the terms of his own times and his own temperament. We are all, as Galsworthy says, little bits of continuity, and "the still sad music of humanity" remains the same melody, whether we listen to it as the Song of Solomon or in the latest jazz tempo, interpreted through shawm or lyre, spinet or saxophone.

All art, since it cannot use as its material anything but what already exists in the universe, must in some degree be a comment and interpretation of that universe, but literature has a relationship to life far more close than that of any of the other arts, since it uses the same medium by whose help we carry on our human intercourse, the medium of language. The media of colour, sound, mass or line are not used as natural bases for human communication except in the world of the cinema, where the art of miming and making faces must perforce replace human speech. Average human beings live their lives with the help of words, conveying their experiences, expressing their thoughts, and interpreting their emotions through them. The literary artist uses exactly the same material, hence the impossibility of detaching the experiences of literature entirely from those of actual living. Oscar Wilde declares that, to the elect, beautiful things mean only Beauty, but I think we can safely say that there is no human being to whom *Hamlet* or the *Odyssey* means only Beauty. The artistic emotion the most cultivated and sensitive mind experiences on reading them, is complicated by direct emotional, intellectual and moral impressions which it inevitably receives at the same time.

More than ever is this so with the novel, since the novel is almost entirely concerned with problems and situations common to all men, so that it is more than ever inevitable that questions of content alone should intrude in our judgment of it, as well as the aesthetic questions of the fusion of subject matter and form. The novel, dealing as it does with the actions and passions of human beings whom we think of in the terms of fellow living creatures, and telling of crisis, incident, character and circumstance within the observation of us all, is bound to express certain of the moral values men live by, and by implication, if not directly, the attitude of the author towards those values, so that it is about as difficult to divorce a discussion of the novel from questions of conduct as for a blind man with one arm to get out of a bunker with a toothpick—as Mr. P. G. Wodehouse would say!

But this brings us at once to the central difficulty of intelligent appreciation of the modern English and American novel, and the ground of attack by the intellectuals and the aesthetes. Human life, as all experiencers of it are agreed, is a sorry scheme. We are all comrades in distress and dissatisfaction, united in a tragic community of longing to lighten "the weary weight of all this unintelligible world." Hence, since the novel portrays so many of the riddles of life as we meet them in life itself, great numbers of readers go to the novel in much the same spirit in which they would go to a fortune teller. They do not really want to be told the truth about life, or to listen to speculation about life, they want to be reassured about it: to get some comforting "message." There is a certain American magazine which sends out slips for its contributors' guidance, stating: "Humour, tragedy and pathos are acceptable, but not stories that are morbid or that leave the reader uncomfortable." The editor of this magazine reads the average reader aright. Hence the inanities of the ordinary magazine story and the glut of popular love romances, where, in place of the pessimism "more black than ash buds in the front of March" (which is so popular among the intellectuals, but which leaves the average reader uncomfortable), we find a sincere sentimentalism more sticky than chestnut buds in the front of April, which apparently somehow convinces him, and still more, her, that she herself some day will be clothed with the heavens and crowned with the stars.

This craving for a certain emotional effect from fiction goes deeper than the demand for sentimental romance, and involves the whole matter of "uplift." There is, says Mr. Edwin Muir, one great orthodox heresy about the universe which makes it such a dull place to live in, and that is the dogma that if a thing is not useful it cannot be important. It is a heresy embedded with peculiar tenacity in the Anglo-Saxon mind, which makes it demand perpetually that the meaning of life and the message of art shall lie in its own especial code of conduct, and which makes it distrust any manifestation of human energy unless a definite lesson can be drawn from it. Readers who hold this heresy seem to regard literature as the Polonius of life, a sort of mine of useful and helpful and improving maxims and truisms, whose sole purpose is to be the mouthpiece of established order and the bourgeois virtues: the missing link between God and suburbia. It arises from a failure to distinguish between literary and moral values, between conduct in life and the representation of conduct in writing. Now this *is* difficult for the general reader, because as I have already said it is not possible entirely to divorce literature from moral questions. There is, of course, always the extreme logical position of Plato, the first Puritan, who argued that since art is imitation, and of bad no less than good, therefore there must be evil in it: that the same person cannot at the same time devote himself to the development of pure good and be creating characters of evil. Hence his ideal republic must banish entirely all art and all artists. But if we accept the Aristotelian view that the universe is rationally organized, and that the existence of art in it as one of the natural functions of human nature proves that it has a proper place in life and a part in the ultimate perfection of life, we must decide what that place is. "You confuse two things," says Tchekov, "solving a problem, and stating it correctly. It is only the second that is obligatory for the artist." This is the whole kernel of the matter. When the artist is creating he no more thinks of the purely moral qualities of his creation than passionate lovers think of the moral qualities of the child that may spring from their ecstatic union. Creation is creation, not something else. The artist takes as much pains and is as much absorbed in his creation of evil as of good, of ugliness as of beauty. He lavishes as much work and care, and exactly the same *sort* of work and care, on Iago as on Othello, on Medea as on Alkestis, on a gargoyle as on the Venus of Milo. He looks upon experience as an end in itself, while the moralist regards it as a symptom which must be treated in relation to some general manifestation of truth, and requires that a book shall conform to some special ethical formula. We might illustrate the point from that very brilliant recent novel, from which I have already quoted, *The Constant Nymph*. The implacable reporter of human experience who is the creator of that book chooses a group of human beings to play her story, notes the inevitable outcome of the clashes of character and circumstance she has planned, and is concerned only to present that interplay of character and circumstance with all the intensity of realization, clarity of outline, and economy of language of which she is capable. *She has no other aim*. Were she a sentimentalist we should be presented with an Ethel M. Dell or a Maud Diver solution and Florence would have a convenient railway accident so that Teresa could marry Lewis Dodd and live happily ever afterwards. Sentimental readers, no doubt, wish this had happened. Or again, if she were a social moralist, like the late Mrs. Humphry Ward, Lewis would conform his music to the immediate claims of his environment, and we should have an end typifying Art rendering Service to Humanity through the Sacrifice of Selfish Aims. And social moralists, no doubt, wish *that* had happened. But as it is the book stands as a piece of literature and must be discussed as such. It is neither a dream nor a tract.

To say that a serious novel must be discussed as a piece of creative art and not as a piece of life is not to contradict what we have already said as to the impossibility of divorcing the discussion of literature from questions of conduct. The novel is concerned with the statement of human truths and problems and cannot get away from them, but the point always to be remembered is that the author is concerned with the *creation* of those truths and problems and not primarily with any *comment* on them. The illustrations of conduct which he creates concern us (in our character as critics of literature) only in so far as they involve a criticism of the *literary* treatment of such conduct, and an understanding of the author's mind. It is just as much a sin against *literature* to read a book for nothing but a useful moral lesson, as to read it for nothing but a sensual thrill, and to judge a work to be defective *as literature* because it leaves no helpful message and encouragement for living, is as stupid as to judge a chrysanthemum to be defective because it does not eat as well as a cauliflower.

Perhaps the point will be clearer if we again look for a moment at the past and consider some accepted masterpieces and our attitude to them. We shall then be aware at once that our enjoyment of them depends not at all on our agreement or disagreement with their ethical standards. Since public opinion is now agreed about the artistic value of these works, we instinctively leave any personal view of their morality out of account in reading them and concentrate our attention on feeling their literary qualities. For example, suppose we found this paragraph in the police news of a daily paper:

MIXED MARRIAGE. MURDER AND SUICIDE

Finds Truth Too Late, Says Colored Husband

An inquest was held on Wednesday last to investigate the circumstances attending the deaths of a Moor and his wife (a white woman) which took place on Monday night last under tragic circumstances. It appeared from the evidence of the deceased man's secretary, Michael Cassio, that the couple, who had only recently been married, had lived together very happily, until his employer had come under the influence of his manager, a man of the name of Iago. This man, who was now in hospital as the result of wounds received on the night of the murder, had convinced his employer of his wife's improper intimacy with himself (the witness). Inflamed by his jealousy, and without waiting to carefully investigate the charge, the Moor had suffocated his wife in bed, and on discovering from her maid that his suspicions had been groundless, had stabbed himself to death in the presence of the police who were about to take him into custody.

On reading this sordid tale of lust and jealousy we should probably comment on the problems of the marriages of mixed races and the baseness of human instincts, and so on: if it appeared as a modern novel, the American Society for the Suppression of Vice would certainly try to get it suppressed, and a great number of readers would say they didn't want to hear about that sort of people and that life was unpleasant enough without meeting that sort of thing in fiction. But when we read the play of *Othello* we are not concerned to discuss the facts of the plot as such, because we allow ourselves to be concerned with the vitality of Shakespeare's imagination in dealing with them: the literary and not the moral question. Or again, the fact that there are very few people nowadays who would agree with Milton's theology or believe literally the story of *Paradise Lost* does not impair our literary enjoyment of the epic. In the same way Shelley's *Prometheus Unbound* can be fully appreciated by some one who is neither a socialist nor a pantheist: Burns's *Jolly Beggars* can be read with pleasure by a member of the Charity Organization Society, and Cowley's delightful lines on drinking not only by any citizen of the United States in general, but I believe by even the strictest inhabitant of Kansas! It will be found, indeed, that none of us demands standards of use from accepted works of art: we do not ask the cubic contents of Keats's Grecian Urn, or require that Shelley's West Wind shall grind corn.

It is time, though, to leave the negative discussion of what intelligent criticism is not, and to attempt to form some standard of what it is: to try to answer that continually recurring and teasing question of what to look for in a book, and how the average man and woman can get all that can be got out of his or her general reading.

Appreciation depends on partnership, on the establishment of understanding between writer and reader. "What is a book?" says Anatole France. "A series of little printed signs, essentially only that. It is for the reader himself to supply the forms and colours and sentiments to which these signs correspond. It will depend on him whether the book be dull or brilliant, hot with passion or cold as ice." It is true that the reader gets what he deserves out of a book. As we have seen. the writer of a novel is trying to interpret something of human existence as it appears to his temperament, to give some created vision of what life seems to him to be. At the same time the reader unconsciously contributes his own view and his own personality, and the result of the fusion is criticism. And there are always two main positions from which criticism springs. On the one hand the reader's view of his partnership with the writer may be that it should merely supply a duplication of his own ideas. He may desire, not a stimulus to further thought, but certainty, an assurance about his own pre-established codes of decision, which shall make any further search for reality unnecessary to him. Or, on the other hand, he may possess the experiencing faculty, the love of mental and emotional adventure for its own sake, the knowledge that there is always something to be discovered about the world we live in, that it must necessarily be larger than any one view of it, and that to have an ardour for such discovery is to make life full of an inexhaustible interest. Such a reader will not be concerned only with the sort of people and the sort of conventions and codes to which he is accustomed and of which he approves. He is not a Puritan, but he loves *The Pilgrim's Progress;* not a sentimentalist, but he delights in the analysis of *Clarissa;* not a libertine, but a happy reader of Byron; not a Catholic, but enraptured by *The Hound of Heaven;* not a Jew, but profoundly stirred by the drama of Job and Jehovah. And although he has likes and dislikes, he makes them give an account of themselves; using his intellectual faculties to make his criticism self-conscious, aware of itself, and of the reason for its pleasures and rebellions. "A good hater" if need be, but not a mere helpless victim of prejudice.

From this latter position springs Taste. In other words, to have a gusto for life is its essential root. To be able, with Fielding, to address humanity as "thou jolly substance." Art is communication of experience; the novel is direct communication of human experience, and the fascination of its study lies first of all in an unquenchable and detached curiosity to meet and appraise as many as possible of the multitudinous existing varieties of character, situation, action and opinion. It follows, then, that from the emotional and intellectual point of view, the matter of supreme importance in criticizing a novel is the answer to the question: from what kind of mind does this writing come? Out of how deep and wide an experience was it born? This, and not the mere question of the subject-matter, is the all-important starting point for discussion. Here again, perhaps, illustrations are best first from literary classics. Let us take Shakespeare's tragedies. Judged merely as a picture of human existence, nothing could be more ghastly than the spectacle of the cosmos they present. We see innocence murdered and trust betrayed, cruelty torturing old age and treachery triumphing over honesty. Nobility, courage, generosity, truth, are dashed to pieces under the wheels of Fate. Man, struggling in the grip of circumstance and character, is beaten in that struggle every time. Evil always triumphs over good: Iago is proved stronger than Othello and Desdemona, Goneril and Regan vanquish Lear, Hamlet is overthrown, so is Brutus, so is Antony, so is poor young Romeo. Yet the flavour of life which is left on the mental palate after reading Shakespeare is not that of the despair which a play like Galsworthy's *Justice*, for instance, leaves, but something much nearer exaltation—a very strange effect to be produced by the spectacle of the world's illusion! Shakespeare's mind being rich, sure, intense, powerful and comprehensive, it is the impress of the qualities of richness, sureness, intensity, power and understanding which is left upon the mind of the reader. The same magic is achieved by Hardy, whose mind is such that his treatment of the mockery of life and the ignoble bludgeonings of Fate, his picture of this "show God ought surely to shut up soon," becomes a thing of grandeur, its pettiness transmuted into dignity, its baseness ennobled. If again we look at the world with the eyes and mind of George Moore, we see it as a place for little more than varied opportunities for various kinds of sensation; if we look at it with Shaw we see it from the point of view of inspired common sense; if we look at it with Dickens, from that of inspired common sensibility. Coming to the modern novel, we can illustrate the same truth by seeing the various ways in which one theme can be treated by different personalities. Let us take that ever-popular situation in fiction, the theme of illicit love. The moralist will simply disapprove of any novel dealing with an "unpleasant theme," and dismiss it at that. The possessor of taste, very well aware that it is a part of life and cannot be ignored so easily, is interested to mark all the tones and degrees of its representation in the terms of various mentalities. He can see it handled by a detached artistic mind like Arnold Bennett or Rose Macaulay or Willa Cather; or by a pictorial mind like Hergesheimer; or by a scientific, analytic mind like Shaw or Wells; or a pitiful, gentle mind like Galsworthy; or a sincerely sentimental mind like A. S. M. Hutchinson, or a cynically sentimental mind like Michael Arlen; or a commonplace and rather base mind, as is usual in any of the Legs and Lingerie School; or perhaps one might say, by a vacuum in place of a mind, as is usual in any of the writers of sentimental romances.

Individual preferences must always exist, in literature as in life, and they have to be accepted in the same spirit. Just as sometimes we simply cannot understand how our friends choose their mates as they do, so, maybe, we cannot understand what they see in, say Miss Dorothy Richardson. It does not really help matters, however, to echo Dr. Johnson as he discussed a book with Boswell, and to bellow as if it were a convincing argument, "You, sir, may think it excellent, but that does not make it so." Tastes differ, and if you are all for steak and onions, caviar and peaches is unsatisfying. Beyond opinion about the merits of individual writers, there are always the two great types of mind which we label Romantic and Realistic. When all the recent criticism which argues against the academic exactitude of the labels has been accepted, there still remain two types of mind, and most readers have a bias towards one or the other. Some naturally prefer looking through magic casements opening on the foam of perilous seas in faëry lands forlorn: their Pegasus is like that of Edward Lear's old Person of Bazing,

> Whose presence of mind was amazing,
> He purchased a steed,
> Which he rode at full speed
> And escaped from the people of Bazing.

(A poem which might stand as a symbolist rendering of that literature of escape the psychologists tell us so much about.) This class of readers generally regards the novels of Jane Austen or of Ethel Sidgwick or of Trollope or of Arnold Bennett, much as du Maurier's Frenchman regarded the fox-hunt, "no promenade, no band of music, nossing," while to those who enjoy that kind of thing the commonplace brings its own excitement and thrill, and a book like Walter de la Mare's *Memoirs of a Midget*, or Cabell's tales of romance, and stories in general of "elves, fairies and such like mummery," as Fielding would say, are about as comforting as a cold crumpet. It is useless to argue about it, because the extremists on either side cannot understand each other, just as the mystic cannot understand the cynic's profound indifference to inner realities, and the intellectual ironist cannot understand any one really bothering much about the soul. The critic can only follow that excellent advice, "Do not call the tortoise unworthy because she is not something else," and recognize the fact, true again in literature as in life, that it is quite possible to have a detached admiration without affection and complete sympathy.

So much for the human appeal of the novel and its capacity to satisfy the human curiosity of its readers. That curiosity is the essential basis of all enjoyment of fiction, but it is not possible fully to appreciate it without a further quality—the sense of craftsmanship and style. The difference between art and life is one of Form. Every day of our existence we meet, and realize quite well that we meet, both in our own lives and in those of others, the materials for drama or fiction. But the experiences of living are blurred and confused by a mass of superfluous detail and dialogue, by a bewildering medley of extraneous character and action, which interfere constantly with the development and statement of any single situation. To try to report the thoughts, speech and activities of one single day in a man's life has spread over nearly a thousand pages of print in *Ulysses*. The function of art is to select, clarify and isolate the experiences of life within a certain form. "Life is like a blind and limitless expanse of sky, forever dividing into tiny drops of circumstance that rain down, thick and fast, a ceaseless, meaningless drip. Art is like the dauntless plastic force that builds up stubborn, amorphous substance cell by cell into the frail geometry of a shell." This subject will be treated at greater length in a later chapter and now it is enough to say that in the novel this means bringing character, situation, point of view, setting and background under the discipline of outline, enclosing both the raw material and the creative vision of the artist towards his material in a certain structure of expression. Critics of the novel in textbooks which profess to teach novel-writing in twelve lessons (or words to that effect), often speak as if there were a right or wrong form for the novel. This cannot be. The purpose of the serious novel (I mean a novel which is a serious piece of literary work, though it may be a pure comedy) is to give interest and enjoyment to the reader—not the merely superficial enjoyment and interest of something which amuses him when he is tired, but the true enjoyment of having his faculties energized and vitalized by being called into play in a comparison of the experience of another mind with that of his own. That novel is a good novel which succeeds in communicating vividly the writer's experience, and there can be no rules for what form succeeds in doing that— except the rule of success! We might quote Mr. Kipling on tribal lays, and apply the same remark to the novel.

> There are nine and sixty ways of constructing tribal lays.
> And every single one of them is right.

The novelist may convey his effect by the rambling, enormously patient reporting of James Joyce in *Ulysses*, or by the rigid selection of Willa Cather in *A Lost Lady*, by the architectural massiveness of Arnold Bennett's *The Old Wives' Tale* or by the brilliant impressionism of Aldous Huxley's *Antic Hay*. He may be as direct as Wells or as elusive as Virginia Woolf: he may set chronology at defiance as in *Lord Jim*, or he may make the lives of a group of characters centre in one night as in *Nocturne:* he may make his action live at four removes from the teller of the tale, as when, in *Chance*, we listen to what Marlow said that Mrs. Fyne said that Flora said the governess said, or he may be as frankly autobiographical as Samuel Butler in *The Way of All Flesh*. Provided that the reader feels that he simply must finish the book, the novelist has succeeded in his aim and his form has justified itself.

The Novel and the Age

The Novel and the Age

I suppose what I am trying to render is nothing more nor less than Life—as one man has found it. I want to tell—*myself*, and my impressions of the thing as a whole, to say things I have come to feel intensely of the laws, traditions, usages, and ideas we call society, and how we poor individuals get driven and lured and stranded among these windy, perplexing shoals and channels.

GEORGE PONDEREVO in *Tono Bungay* describes here very well something of the experience of every serious novelist. The novel is inevitably contemporary social history; it inevitably reflects the society from which the novelist creates. It is true that there are always those who declare that this is an error, that the books which live are the books which express, not the current ideas and attitudes, either positive or negative, but the personalities of writers, and that there is, therefore, no such thing as a "trend" in literature. But though personality is a skin that no writer can slip, whatever he may write about: though it is a shadow which walks inexorably by his side, so also is the age he lives in. Whatever subject he takes, he cannot but express one in terms of the other, he can escape from neither. Every age has its own flavour. Nietzsche said that all life was a dispute about Taste and Tasting, and it is that eternal dispute which seasons each epoch in literary and social history. We recognize the distinctive taste on the mental palate by appropriately descriptive adjectives: we call the Elizabethan age spacious, the Augustan urbane, the Victorian smug, and we instinctively feel that none of these epithets gives any sense of the savour of our own time. Yet we also have an inherent sense that there is such a savour around us to-day, and we feel it especially in the novel, since so much of the social thought and feeling of the present day distils itself in the form of fiction.

The interest for the observant reader is to mark the variety of ways in which personality expresses itself in this field and to distinguish between the conscious and unconscious reflections of the spirit of the age. For certain novelists very definitely exploit contemporary atmosphere and interest for their own profit. I do not mean "best sellers." They are not generally of this class. Their popularity is the result of their unconscious appeal to the average mentality, and since the average mentality in any age is sentimental and superficial, the most popular writers are the Ethel M. Dells and A. S. M. Hutchinsons who make fiction to that pattern. But it is not by taking thought that any one can write best sellers. They are penned with the heart's blood: it is the passionate cry of mediocrity to mediocrity, shallow calling unto shallow. The exploitation of the present I mean is more subtle, and is the cause of the "dated" book. I do not suggest, of course, that a book dealing with a contemporary problem need necessarily be dated. There are very few, if any, human problems, which are merely contemporary, and any writer profoundly and genuinely concerned with a contemporary problem is usually found to be concerned with its universal application as well. *Mr. Britling Sees It Through,* for instance, is not really "dated" in its main subject—that of a keen and sensitive mind suddenly faced with emotional realities never before experienced: or *Main Street* again, while it attacks modern midwestern American small-town life, satirizes the provincial spirit the whole world over. These books reflect the spirit of the age by making us acutely conscious of a contemporary facet of some general human truth. But there is a competent, clever group of modern novelists whose aim and achievement is much more restricted. They are professional writers and they make it their business to know what the public wants: what degree of daringness in subject and treatment will attract and not disgust: what spice of scandal and sauce of shock will allure and not offend: how to introduce as many as possible of the liveliest topics of the hour, and to make them as lively and immediate as may be. And so we get our chronicles of the contemporary political, ecclesiastical, literary, theatrical, and social sets, the new literary popularity of the oldest profession, the problems of adolescence, marriage, maternity, sex, the generations, war, education, psychology, and religion, acted by a company of thoroughly up-to-date young men and women, ex-soldiers, heartless hussies, cads, cats, frequenters of night clubs, stage favourites, the clergy, journalists, financiers, and smart talkers, all concerned with the aspects of the present-day questions which the superficially cultivated bourgeoisie discuss at their dinner tables. They are of little interest to the intelligent student of either literature or society, for they are ineffectual both as artists and as critics. It is not from the Compton Mackenzies, Stephen McKennas, W. L. Georges, Michael Arlens, and Alec Waughs of the day, or even from the courteous drawing-room Hugh Walpoles, that we feel the essential character and the peculiar vitality of our own time. These writers imitate the age, they do not express it, and their epitaph has been written by Robert Graves in a quatrain:

EPITAPH ON AN UNFORTUNATE ARTIST

He found a formula for drawing comic rabbits.
This formula for drawing comic rabbits paid.
So in the end he could not change the tragic habits
This formula for drawing comic rabbits made.

Yet the pervasive sense of a new epoch is over the present, felt in the work of every serious artist or social chronicler of the times. The stories and situations in their writings may be old, for there are really very few stories and situations in life, but as they are re-told and recast, the influence and modification of a new grouping of moral and mental criteria create a new

spirit and a new outlook. Who can say whether it is
literature which changes life, or life which changes
literature? They are inextricably interrelated and in-
teractive. The writer surveys the life around him with
his creative vision and thought, and pictures it as his
personality sees it: but at the same time the public is
doing its thinking and feeling in crowds: its members
are reading the same books and are being swayed by
the powers of mass conformity and mass rebellion about
them, with the result that life holds up the mirror to
fiction every bit as much as fiction reflects life. Anyhow, the change is here. The Victorian age, like the
Cheshire Cat, has faded out to an optimistic shadow,
and we find ourselves in what a good many commen-
tators assure us is the Age of Disillusion. We can
illustrate the position very well from two of Max
Beerbohm's cartoons. One represents *The Future, as
Beheld by the Nineteenth Century* and shows a solid,
prosperous, bewhiskered John Bull, full-fed on Jeremy
Bentham, contemplating an enlarged edition of himself
with amiable self-satisfaction and approval. In the
next picture, *The Future as Beheld by the Twentieth
Century*, we have a lanky, fearful unhappy looking
youth, with a black band on his arm, timidly regarding
a large question mark on a dim and cloudy background.
The reaction from the Victorian standard can hardly
go further than it has gone to-day. It is, presumably,
the natural swing of the pendulum. The idols of one
age generally become the skittles of the next, the fame

of yesterday's immortal puts on mortality to-day, and while one part of the human mind enjoys building altars to new gods, another part enjoys knocking the noses off old statues. When Jane Austen was left in charge of her sister's garden, she wrote after a few weeks, "I will not say your mulberry trees are dead, but I am afraid they are not alive," and the contemporary reputations of the great Victorians are somewhat in the condition of the mulberry trees.

The moderns attack the Victorians because they appear to them self-complacent. They think of Mr. Roebuck exclaiming: "I look round me and ask, What is the state of England? I ask you whether the world over, or in past history, there is anything like it? Nothing! I pray God that our unrivalled happiness may last." The moderns are apt to forget that most of the great Victorians also attacked their own age for the same reason, but in spite of that, it is certainly true that, as we look back on it from the present, the main body of intelligent public opinion in the Victorian age seems to us to have been solidly sure of itself. That is the great difference, as Max Beerbohm points out pictorially, between the past age and the present. The Victorian novel shared in the general self-confidence. The novelists all hold a certain established code of moral and social order, as if in all sincerity they believed that it embodied ultimate truth. Though they create character with abundance of vigour and vitality, they all accept this moral and social pattern as a matter of course. They all regard the inhabitants of the rest of Europe as inferior and slightly ridiculous: servants are either pathetic or comic, and the wealthy bourgeoisie are almost always vulgar. Sexual morals are judged by a rigid and unswerving code. Little Em'ly's whole life is ruined because she has been seduced by Steerforth, Jane Eyre's love must be frustrated until Rochester's lunatic wife is safely in cinders. Good and evil are quite obvious and very easily recognized: there is an absolute standard which is accepted by all as the correct standard. Though in life all proof of the ultimate truth of this standard must have rested on faith, it was not so in fiction. There poetic justice always triumphed, good was suitably rewarded and evil suitably punished, and it would be inconceivable to imagine a Victorian hero dismissed to a life and death like Lord Jim's, or left at the end of a novel in the position of young Jon Forsyte in Galsworthy's *To Let*.

Every age, as it lives, regards itself, I suspect, as peculiarly an age of change. Take this morsel of dialogue:

"You see," said Dr. Jenkinson, "the age we live in is an age of change."

"But this age," said Leslie, "is peculiar surely in the extraordinary rapidity of its changes, and this has plunged us into a state of mental anarchy that has not been equalled since mental order was known. There is no recognized rule of life anywhere. . . . All society it seems to me is going to pieces."

And this is not a fragment from a novel by H. G. Wells, but part of the dinner table conversation in *The New Republic* published in those dead Victorian days of 1877! When we look back on the past we win a certain sense of proportion: we see the whole process of the growth, development, flower and decay of movements and ideas, and in consequence we lose that sense of the flux and welter of change, of conflicting opinion and embattled thought which jar us into consciousness as we live in its midst. To-day we are all convinced again that we are living with revolution all around us, and the faith of the Victorian novelist seems as dead as that of the Greek dramatists. Though there must be an immensely wide demand among the general public for some specific religious assurances in place of the decay of Victorian dogma—a demand which can be illustrated by the number of conversions claimed by the Catholic Church, or again by the startling figures of the sales of Papini's *Life of Christ*, this side of the modern consciousness does not appear at all in the serious modern novel. On the contrary it has become a commonplace of criticism nowadays to say that the civilized modern writer is a disillusioned pessimist. I would call him rather agnostic than pessimist, for the standpoint of the intelligent modern seems to rest more on doubt than on a conviction of evil triumphant. It is simply that he questions profoundly the confident and somewhat glib assurances of the old standard truth. As far as the universe is concerned he feels that, with every discovery in knowledge, we find that we know less and less about it. We realize, as is suggested by a passage in *Those Barren Leaves*, that the body exists simultaneously in various parallel worlds: to the artist in form and colour: to the physicist in terms of electrons: to the chemist in architectural molecules: to the biologist as a tissue of cells: to the moralist as an instrument for good and evil. But this realization brings us no nearer an understanding of the relationship, if any, between these parallel existences. We simply do not know the secrets of the universe we inhabit, and the civilized modern does not pretend to know.

This uncertainty which meets his mind on every side has revolutionized his moral outlook. His moral values have shifted: the outlines of the vices and the virtues have lost their firmness: he no longer pretends to find existence emotionally intelligible. Life refuses to make any absolute statements; it remains infinitely formidable and perverse, an implacable and impenetrable force without any apparent symmetry or design. This atmosphere is everywhere in Conrad, saturating his work with that peculiarly pervasive ironic perplexity of his, or again it is the most powerful impression left by perhaps the most interesting novel of 1924, E. M. Forster's *A Passage to India*. Here we are profoundly sensible of the vast muddling energy of the cosmos, spawning into millions upon millions of futile human creatures. We have the most acute observation of the conversational inanities, the mental disorder, the emotional delusions of these human creatures, with abrupt flashes when we become conscious of the impingement of the enormous forces of the universal—forces felt by some of the human actors, but not apprehended or understood by any one. As Miss Quested and Mr. Fielding talk together for the last time, they reach the end of their spiritual tether almost at once: their thought about the experience they have passed through is all ragged, unfinished, meaningless: they simply feel helplessly baffled. As they state their little personal conclusions, "Anyhow I want to go on living" or "I don't believe in God," they have a sensation of themselves as "dwarfs, talking, shaking hands and assuring themselves that they stood on the same footing of insight," while all about them is the vast uncharted unknown. All comment by them must be pure conjecture—"Perhaps life is a mystery not a muddle. . . . They could not tell, they had not the apparatus for judging."

Here is the type of the intelligent modern, seeing the world as Calamy saw it from his mountain hut in Aldous Huxley's *Those Barren Leaves,* "beautiful, terrible and mysterious, pregnant with what enormous secret, symbol of what formidable reality?" Himself sensitive, alert, anxious, but forced at present to conclude that he has not as yet the material with which to form a definite decision.

The same exploratory spirit is everywhere among the literary thinkers. Pirandello with his obsession about reality and illusion: Cabell with his suggestive negative decision that the ultimate magic of all desire, and pursuit, physical or mental, lies in the inaccessibility of the thing desired and pursued; D. H. Lawrence, shedding skin after skin of his intellectual and emotional positions in his almost frantic search for some conclusion, some creed, some code on which to repose— some outline into which life can be enclosed, while at the same time accepting the validity of all its facts. "Man is a Thought Adventurer," he says, and that might be a motto for much serious modern fiction, but its adventures have no conclusion or finality. The twentieth century novel, indeed, might almost be identified with that device of punctuation so liberally employed by its creators, and called the Novel of the Three Dots. . . . It suggests, inquires, collects instances, supplies illustrations on every side of human experience, but it would fain leave all ultimate judgment tailing off into impartial indecision.

This hesitation and uncertainty of spiritual outlook, which is what the older generation find so uncomfortable in the modern novel, accompanies a relentless frankness towards actualities which distresses it still more. For though the final beliefs of the mentally alive minority who make the world of serious fiction are so vague, though it is so unwilling to hold any happy conviction of a beneficent cosmic order, it is laden with a most unhappy conviction of the cosmic *dis*order which it can see with its own eyes and judge with its own mind. "The condition of the world is on the nerves of the young," says some one in *The White Monkey*, and it needs no criticism to point out the irritated perception of the falsity and futility of accepted standards, and the exasperated refusal to continue to accept them, which have infected almost the entire young intelligentsia. As Lilly says in *Aaron's Rod*: "We simply will not face the world as we've made it, and our souls as we find them. We'll never get anywhere till we stand up . . . and face *everything* out, and break the old forms." It is advice which the present generation of novelists have followed in many varying fashions. Sometimes, as with D. H. Lawrence himself, it is with a kind of violent and windy horror and despair at the hopeless impossibility of finding truth, either in his own emotional nature, or in anything else in the universe. Or there is the elegant ruthlessness of Katherine Mansfield, or of Stella Benson, as she probes the self-conscious insincerity of her heroine Ipsie in *Pipers and a Dancer*.

For real women love was the tree on which the fruit of life was hung; for Ipsie love was a spray of peach blossom in a fine wind. It had no root in her. Nothing that she knew, nothing that she desired seemed really rooted in her. Love for her was compounded of small blossoming pleasures, the pleasure of gratified vanity, the desire for experience, the determination to miss nothing that others possessed, the excitement of untried mental intimacy, intoxicating insecurity, the pleasures her eyes took in faces, a thrilling pain in the diaphragm in the presence of a man—these were her

pleasures in love. There was, she realized, something missing—*given* love was missing. Whenever she realized this
she felt cruelly defrauded, and loathed herself.

Or there is the boisterous realism of Sinclair Lewis,
showing up the myth and moonshine of the business
world or the medical profession: or the good-humoured
satire of Gerhardi's *Futility:* or again the robust sanity
of Rose Macaulay in *Potterism* or *Dangerous Ages*, exposing hypocrisy wherever she finds it, in stupid old
age or callow youth, in politics, in journalism, in old
prejudices or new fads. E. M. Delafield has more
venom, but the same spirit, and we can see it again in
May Sinclair's pitiless dissection of Canon Chamberlain
or Mr. Waddington; in Hugh Walpole's *The Cathedral;*
in the hero of Lady Russell's *Vera* and the heroine of
S. G. Millin's *Mary Glenn;* in the exquisite draughts-
manship which portrays Gerald Poynard in Elinor
Wylie's *Jennifer Lorn,* and in portraits such as Willa
Cather's *A Lost Lady* or Ethel Sidgwick's *Laura* or
Mary Thriplow in *Those Barren Leaves.*

There is the same tearing away of specious and
plausible disguises, the same determination to "face
everything out" in the modern treatment of special
themes. Just as the novelists exhibit an almost brutal
candour in unmasking individual counterfeit human
beings, so do they expose mercilessly the shallow
thinking and feeling behind the conventional attitudes
towards collective human problems. The Church, the
Empire, social injustice, political theory, domestic mo-

rality, all are openly reviewed and examined with a direct and unashamed outspokenness. Unpalatable actualities are no longer to be evaded; facts have got to be faced. Society must realize that war is not glorious and noble, but filthy and futile, that imperialism produces bigotry and greed; that parents and children almost always disagree; that men get tired of their wives, and wives of their husbands; that the unmarried girl is not necessarily chaste; that the Church is as insincere as the laity, and that Politics and Business and Education and Finance and the Press are all corrupt, and ruled first and foremost by self-interest.

Iconoclasm is not a discovery of the twentieth century, nor have the moderns a monopoly in looking facts in the face. Another glance at *The New Republic*, indeed, shows us Mr. Storks claiming as the noble and peculiar feature of 1877 "a universal, intrepid, dogged resolve to find out and face the complete truth of things, and to allow no prejudice to obscure our vision." Moreover, though scepticism springs from a healthy revulsion from cant, it is a perverse and intractable doctrine in its developments. The degradation of emotion in sentimental romance and the desire to avoid themes staled by commonplace handling, a disgust at the unthinking acceptance of conventional situations in the place of the integrity of experience, these are at the root of the modern rebellion against tradition. It is the fear of uplift which has made writers afraid of rapture: they distrust wings lest they should soar into the Way of an Eagle, and prefer the bondage of cynicism to This Freedom. But it is none the less a dangerous frame of mind. In their anxiety to avoid the commonplace some writers seem to have confused individuality of vision with exaggeration of statement: they have been as fearful of moderation as of mediocrity, and have proved themselves as much the slaves of public opinion as the sentimentalists. For there are two ways of being a slave to convention, and the man who is afraid ever to agree with it is as much in its grip as the man who is afraid ever to differ from it. The aesthetes are not really much better than the Potterites, and trying to shock your maiden aunt is not originality. We catch an echo of the patter of some of the extremists among the young intelligentsia in *The White Monkey*, where Michael declares that the smart literary set say it well, but have nothing to say and won't last. Fleur is outraged.

"D'you mean to say Sibley isn't going to live?"
"Lord, no!"
"But he's so perfectly sure that almost everybody else is dead or dying. Surely he has critical genius!"

Perhaps the attitude of studied disrespect of the older generation in art and life imposes only on the Fleur Forsytes of the world, but her view illustrates one danger of the superior attitude—the itch to outrage conventional emotion rather than to illustrate genuine emotion in its place, to replace a mechanical conven-

tion with an unconvention which becomes quite as mechanical—and there is another danger in that denial of
all emotion into which the cynic is invariably led. It
is well illustrated in Aldous Huxley's *Antic Hay*, that
cynical and disillusioned satire on modern cynicism and
disillusion, where the limits of cynicism are so mor-
dantly displayed. In this book the superior person has
great fun exposing conventional insincerities and turning the shallow thinking of the general public to his advantage. He can be hilariously comic over modern
publicity methods, he can expose the hypocrisy of
popular ideas of religion and education and can send
a fatally barbed arrow of irony into the heart of the
self-conscious artist. But what then? He can do all
that, but there are certain things he inevitably misses.
He misses all the simple affectionate companionship a
person like Emily can give, and never for a moment can
he capture the spirit in which his architect father builds
his lovely dream city in his attic, or the lively self-suffi-
cient joy which the scholar gets from his Greek. When
he has proved the falseness of what the herd believe in,
he goes on to prove the falseness of what his own set
profess to believe in, and he is left at the end despair-
ingly seeking for any harmony of spirit, face to face
with a universe in which boredom seems to be the only
reality.

"To-morrow," said Gumbril.

"To-morrow," said Mrs. Viveash, "will be as awful as
to-day."

In spite of much that is merely negative, however, even if the achievement of the modern novel towards the elucidation of the modern consciousness (the spirit of the age) had been only what we have already described, it would be something. The agnostic temper of the time has made fiction fearless in experiment, and its spirit of unabashed speculation towards all social and individual problems, and audacious challenge to all accepted conclusions, is in itself of value. Destructive criticism is seldom entirely negative. At least it makes the individual and society self-conscious, aware of facts and positions to which they were not before alive, which is, after all, a starting point for reform. But that is not all. It is, no doubt, to the disadvantage of the novel as a form of art that its concern with the stuff of life as its material almost forces us to include morality in our judgment of it. Each of us is cursed with a Sphinx in his soul asking its perpetual riddle of what is the aim of life, and we instinctively ask of the novelist that he shall help us to answer it. The intelligent reader is no longer contented with the easy emotionalism of the sentimental romance or the arbitrarily accommodating schemes of poetic justice; he finds mere doubt and hesitation a paralysis, and cynicism in the end another name for despair. He is inclined to complain that the modern novel does not get him anywhere (with the exception of Mr. H. G. Wells, who gets him to a different place every time, which comes to the same thing!). But is this true?

Are there not signs and assurances in the contemporary novel of individual faiths and convictions of far greater persuasiveness than any mere traditional tenets? Throughout the last twenty years or so in the history of fiction there have been certain outstanding illustrations of alternative conclusions to a half-hearted conformity with outworn codes: there has been Arnold Bennett's sense of the inwrought dignity which sheer staunchness of character inevitably creates, and of the tremendous basic solidity which the relationship of marriage can give to human existence: there has been Conrad's insistence on honour and loyalty among men as the only root of human solidarity, and Galsworthy's faith, implicit in everything he writes, of fraternity among all living creatures. The dauntless and incessant mind of Wells, as his enemies are continually pointing out, has produced an embarrassment of solutions; but in spite of his mercurial imagination, his millennia all develop from a central inspiration which nothing has ever shaken—his imperishable hope in the Undying Fire, the rebellious god in the heart of man who refuses to allow him to accept his fate meekly. There is, at the conclusion of *Tono Bungay*, a passage on human aspiration which echoes the vague, but none the less profound conviction of the agnostic idealist at all times—a spirit which is felt behind this specifically agnostic age, and which is, I think, making itself heard more and more persistently in the thoughtful novel of to-day. As George Ponderevo sweeps down the Thames in his destroyer, he has a vision of reality comparable to the mystic's ecstasy of knowledge, and through the confusion and futility of modern civilization he sees that *something* drives.

"Something that is at once human achievement and the most inhuman of all existing things. Something comes out of it. . . . How can I express the values of a thing at once so essential and so immaterial?

"I have figured it by the symbol of my destroyer, stark and swift, irrelevant to most human interests. Sometimes I call this reality Science, sometimes I call it Truth. But it is something we draw by pain and effort out of the heart of life, that we disentangle and make clear. Other men serve it, I know, in art, in literature, in social invention, and see it in a thousand different figures, under a hundred names. I see it always as austerity, as beauty. This thing we make clear is the heart of life. It is the one enduring thing. Men and nations, epochs and civilization pass, each making its contribution. . . . It is a something, a quality, an element one may find now in colours, now in sounds, now in thoughts. It emerges from life with each year one lives and feels, and generation by generation and age by age, but the how and why of it are all beyond the compass of my mind. . . ."

The men who follow the promptings of this spirit, and the men who recognize in others its high imperious needs, are those who find reality in this cruel and bewildered world we live in. And it is perhaps significant that the three most stimulating novels of 1925 all emphasize different aspects of this truth: showing three independent and widely divergent creative imaginations

weaving the pattern of life against the same essential
philosophic background.   First Sinclair Lewis in *Arrow-*
smith incarnates the true scientific spirit.

> "To be a scientist—it is not just a different job, so that a
> man should choose between being a scientist and being an
> explorer or a physician or a king or a farmer.   It is a tangle
> of very obscure emotions, like mysticism or wanting to write
> poetry: it makes its victims all different from the good nor-
> mal man.   The normal man, he does not care much what he
> does, except that he should eat and sleep and make love.
> But the scientist is intensely religious. . . ."

His criterion is not the success or failure of his work,
but the doing of it.   He knows he *must* do it, and the
friend who understands him says, "May Koch bless
you," and they are both at the heart of life.   But this
spirit does not dwell only in the patient pursuit of truth
through scientific research; it can be served, as Wells
says, in any manifestation of human creative passion.
Shaw, for instance, illustrates the same power working
through Julius Caesar and through Joan of Arc.   Margaret Kennedy in *The Constant Nymph* shows it working in the artist, wrecking human relationships, tearing
its way through individual suffering and social prejudice, alight in a man who is selfish, undignified and un-
gentle, but who knows with a knowledge beyond human
comprehension, that he is a victim of an inner necessity,
that his vision will compel him with a compulsion to
which he cannot choose but submit.

Finally, in Aldous Huxley's *Those Barren Leaves* there is the brilliant statement of the plea for contemplation. Calamy, writer, lover, cynic, sophisticated man of the twentieth century world, feels within him the birth of the need for unperturbed and untrammelled meditation. Perhaps thought, utterly free and utterly quiet, may bring him to a glimpse of the reality which he feels may lie beyond the limits of ordinary existence. "What bosh you mystics talk," says his friend Cardan, as Calamy struggles to convey his vague hopes. He replies:

"It's only to be expected. How is a man to give an account of something entirely unlike the phenomena of known existence in a language invented to describe these phenomena? You might give a deaf man a most detailed verbal description of the Fifth Symphony; but he wouldn't be much the wiser for it."

"True," said Mr. Cardan; "but I have my doubts whether any amount of sitting under bo-trees really makes it possible for any one to wriggle out of human limitations and get behind phenomena."

"Well, I'm inclined to think that it does make it possible. There we must agree to differ."

Cardan objects again that pure contemplation is negative in the sense that you can really only know yourself in relation to other people, and Calamy replies:

"That's true. Part of yourself you can certainly get to know only in relation to what is outside. In the course of twelve or fifteen years of adult life I think I've got to know that part of me very thoroughly. . . . Why should I go on? . . . On the other hand, there is a whole universe within me, unknown and waiting to be explored; a whole universe that can only be approached by way of introspection and patient uninterrupted thought. Merely to satisfy curiosity it would surely be worth exploring. But there are motives more impelling than curiosity to persuade me. What one may find there is so important that it's almost a matter of life and death to undertake the search."

Again that sense of inner compulsion and vital necessity which must be obeyed, a compulsion and necessity this time which drives the man to renounce the world and the flesh entirely and to seek in ascetic isolation those spiritual verities he dimly apprehends. Chelifer, the rationalist, protests that it is cowardice to run away.

"One has no right to ignore what for ninety-nine out of every hundred human beings is reality. . . . One has no right."

"Why not? One has a right to be six foot nine inches high and to take sixteens in boots. Why hasn't one the right to be born with an unusual sort of mind?"

There are, as Calamy quotes from a Hindu thinker, at least eighty-four thousand ways of achieving the inner harmony which is salvation, and every man has the right to choose any one of them. This then is the positive faith of this age. It may be disillusioned about the faiths and codes of its immediate predecessors, but it has its own doctrine of the right of every soul to find its own salvation: it claims a rational tolerance for all who strive with passion to follow the promptings of heart, mind, or spirit in an effort to elucidate this piece of work which is man.   And although it may, as so many of its critics declare, have its feet in the gutter, it equally has its head among the stars.

Sex Simplexes and Complexes

Sex Simplexes and Complexes

Put *The Innocent Adultery* in *The Whole Duty of Man*.
The Rivals, Act I, Sc. ii.

THE world is not run by thought, nor by imagination,
but by opinion, and though human nature does not
change, social codes and the standards allowed by society to the individual do. The changes are gradual,
for the public always slips into a new point of view
cautiously, like a timid bather taking the water, but
they are nevertheless unmistakable. In our modern
society nowhere are they to be seen more markedly
than in the attitude of the reading public towards the
subject of sex. So all-engrossing has this topic become
that a new connotation has been evolved for the word
itself. "Sex" means literally the quality of distinction
between male and female, but it is a commonplace nowadays to use the word to mean not only that, but the
whole subject of the relationships existing between male
and female, and the relevancy of these relationships to
society in general. This extended meaning of the word
illustrates an enormous development in the interest of
reputable literature on the subject. I say reputable lit-

erature, because, of course, there has never been a time
when pornography has not flourished. The "roguish
French books" which Pepys secretly sniggered over
had, no doubt, as many counterparts in the Victorian
Age as in any other epoch. The change, however, is
in the new frankness with which the cultivated novelists
speak, and the new acceptance of such frankness by the
cultivated reading public, a frankness which can be
illustrated by a recent public meeting, when two young
unmarried women novelists gave a public debate on the
subject of the sex novel. Such an event and all it implies represents a victory over prudery after a struggle
which has been a kind of literary Thirty Years War.
For it was in the nineties that the conflict really became a conscious clash of opinions. It was, I suppose, Scott's prodigious creative gift, thrown on the
side of conventional unreality, which turned the course
of the English novel from the robust acceptance of the
whole of life which we find in the eighteenth century
story-tellers, to the romantic sentimentality of outlook
which mars even the greatest of the mid-Victorian writers of fiction. It was the influence of Zola and of Ibsen which turned it back again into the way of a new
type of realism, and it was in the nineties that the new
battle was joined in England between the forces of this
realism and the old romantic prudery. We can see
from *Locksley Hall Sixty Years After* how angry the
champion of Idyllic morality has been made by the new
trend.

Authors—essayist, atheist, novelist, realist, rhymester, play
  your part,
Paint the mortal shame of nature with the living hues of
  art.

Rip your brothers' vices open, strip your own foul passions
  bare;
Down with Reticence, down with Reverence—forward—
  naked—let them stare!

Feed the budding rose of boyhood with the drainage of your
  sewer,
Send the drain into the fountain, lest the stream should
  issue pure.

And so on. . . . He speaks, too, of the maiden fancies
wallowing in the troughs of Zolaism, while the American critic W. D. Howells declares in 1891 that "all the
women have taken to writing hysterical improprieties."
We find Arthur Waugh in the first number of *The Yellow Book* quoting and criticizing Swinburne's *Dolores*
and protesting that the moderns have reached a degree
of outspokenness which is beyond all decency: "Instead
of leaving these refinements of lust to the haunts to
which they are fitted, it has introduced them into the
domestic chamber and permeated marriage with the
ardours of promiscuous intercourse." But the new
spirit, which was, fundamentally, the scientific spirit,
towards the problems of life, was alive, and full of
youth and zest. It was not *fin de siècle* at all, as the
conservative critics of the nineties supposed, and how-

ever much it was attacked, justly or unjustly, however shocking to Victorian prudery, it was to stand as the most characteristic force in the literature and the society of the coming age. *Esther Waters* and *Tess of the D'Urbervilles* were landmarks on the new way, and the publication of *Jude the Obscure* perhaps the first definite milestone. There for the first time in English letters marriage is recognized as having a reality wholly apart from the mere conventional ceremony which our novelists had always taken it to be.

From then onwards, the history of modern fiction has been the history of more and more frank, unreserved and searching analysis of the truths and mysteries which lurk in the intimate relationships of men and women in "this miserable and naughty world," as the prayer book has it. More and more has Woman been examined honestly as she is, the romantic glorification giving place to the Ibsen and Meredith realist glorification, and thence to the scientific Shavian examination; to May Sinclair's bitter satires on the ideals which could produce completely sterile lives, physically, mentally, emotionally, like that of Harriet Frean, down to the contemporary cynicism of an Aldous Huxley portrait, where the fair sex has turned into the unfair sex.

She was selfish, thirsty for pleasures of the most vulgar sort, liked to bask in an atmosphere of erotic admiration, amused herself by collecting adorers and treating them badly, was stupid and a liar: in other words, was one of the normal types of healthy young womanhood.

Side by side with this frankness about women, it is perhaps natural to find the theme of disillusionment in marriage, of "falling in hate" as one critic calls it, as much a commonplace as the theme of falling in love. *What is home without another?* might be the motto for numbers of novels published every season, and Marvell's *To His Coy Mistress* the text for the whole age:

> The grave's a fine and private place,
> But none, I think, do there embrace.

The decay of Victorian dogma and organized formulae for good and evil, with the general trend towards the holding of individual standards of conduct, is no doubt largely responsible for all this. Swayed for nearly a hundred years by prudish hypocrisy on the subject of sex, English and American society and literature have only recently accepted openly platitudes of existence which have always been regarded as truisms on the Continent: that married men have mistresses and women lovers; that free unions flourish in all walks of society; that sexual abnormalities are common; that women are pursuers and men the pursued; that love is an incident in most men's lives and—if she can get it —almost always "woman's whole existence." All these have been real discoveries for the young people of the present day. Brought up in homes where Victorian repressions and reticences were accepted as a matter of course, the thinking section of the present generation has largely overturned its ideas and codes on reaching maturity. It is little wonder, perhaps, that its spirit of iconoclasm towards its own early prejudices should be thoroughgoing for a space. Convinced that the old meanings attached to life are false, it is determined to see what life *is* before attempting to formulate any new meanings: to experience it to the utmost. As Bunyan's pilgrim ran crying "Life, Life, Eternal Life," the modern pilgrim runs crying, "Life, Life, Immediate Life." Listen to the heroine of a modern novel (of a very bad novel, it is true, but a characteristic one):

"I want everything in life: every pleasure upon earth: good joys, bad joys, cold joys, warm joys, yes, especially the warm joys. I want to experience every kind of emotion, and to know that I, walking the earth, have felt all there is to feel."

The finer artists among the novelists do not make crude statements of this sort, or admire this kind of conscientious Bohemianism, but there is, I think, no single living novelist of the front rank, man or woman, who does not emphasize some special aspect, normal or abnormal, of sexual problems—with greater or lesser frankness according to his or her individual taste, but with no regard at all for the traditional repressions and misrepresentations of the last generation. Galsworthy says of Soames Forsyte: "like most novel readers of his generation, literature coloured his view of life," hence, since at the end of novels the husband always regained the affection of his wife, he felt convinced that Irene's conduct was only the result of a passing phase, and that it would all come right in the end. The moderns are determined that no such facile conventions shall any more be accepted as the truth of life, that they are going to explode all such delusions of the romantic convention. And certainly the banner of the modern novelist is not quartered with prunes and prisms. Wells's heroines lose their virtue with almost the same tiresome consistency with which the Victorian heroines kept theirs; Bennett shows the Pretty Lady as a very human-hearted little professional woman, a type as unlike the traditional courtesan as could well be imagined: Galsworthy lavishes all his tenderest sympathy on the faithless wives who forsake duty for love: Joyce illustrates with brutal frankness the amount of sexual ferment in the hidden consciousness of men and women: D. H. Lawrence shows it as a devouring mania in the lives of his characters: Aldous Huxley bitterly accepts it as the supreme interest in almost all human creatures: Cabell with witty sanity, Hergesheimer with sincere, if somewhat unsophisticated, sincerity, both create the average man's persistent longing for romance, long after youth is past: May Sinclair gives picture upon picture of thwarted sex: Rebecca West turns a charming love story into a study of sex perversion. . . . There is no need to multiply instances: the collective mind of contemporary society is now impregnated with a new consciousness of sex. It has, indeed, become such an obsession with some sections of it, that there are many, as Mr. Edwin Muir humorously remarks, who see the curves of a woman's body in every object not actually flat.

The chief responsibility for this lies with the fashionable pseudo-science of the day, psycho-analysis. The acceptance by a large section of semi-cultivated society of a faith which holds that every single action, conscious or unconscious, which our body or mind commits, has been determined in some degree by the all-comprehensive activity of sex, has very naturally affected profoundly the literary representation of modern society in the novel. There are, first of all, the direct creators of psycho-analytical problems in the form of fiction, resulting in books which fail, I think, without exception, exactly in so far as they are influenced by the new theories, and suffer from this new delirium dreamens, if the pun may be forgiven. D. H. Lawrence, during the phase in which he accepted Freudian dogma, created some extraordinarily unappetizing novels. He showed himself a specialist in the presentation of neurotic and abnormal types (much as Sinclair Lewis, for instance, is a specialist in provincialism in all its aspects), and he assumed a kind of professional air towards the whole subject of sexual excesses, somewhat like that of a superior "mortician" (as the up-to-date undertaker styles himself) towards the subject of corpses. There is the same touch in a great deal of May Sinclair's later work, in many of J. D. Beresford's novels, and in a book like *Cytherea,* while all Rebecca West's distinction of style cannot prevent the sex psychology at the conclusion of *The Judge* from becoming almost comic in its failure to carry any artistic or human conviction.

Apart from the "professional" psycho-analytic fiction, the new license in the presentation and description of sexual phenomena has created a type of "best seller" which is characteristically modern. I have been reading *The Green Hat* in a sincere effort to understand what made it so popular, and I find that Mr. Michael Arlen is helpful in telling us himself, in the person of an imaginary novelist, that the whole purpose of a best seller is to justify a reasonable amount of adultery in the eyes of suburban matrons. "He had observed that in no current English novel was there ever a mention of any woman having a lover because she wanted a lover. She always took a lover because something had upset her, as in real life she might have taken an aspirin." So Mr. Arlen invented Iris Storm as a lady who takes lovers because she wants them, but in order to please the suburban matrons, her life of complete sexual promiscuity and the fact that she never has a single thought or impulse unconnected with her sexual emotions, is justified by a secret single spiritual love, an entirely ridiculous quixotic suppression of truth about the character of her first husband, and a nearly fatal illness in a French convent after the still-birth of her illegitimate child. Luckily her second husband left her lots of money, so the suburban matrons don't have to swallow her being "kept" by any of her lovers, while at the same time she is free to join in the excitingly naughty doings of the smart set. In fact, in sentimental unreality it is all pure Ethel M. Dell and A. S. M. Hutchinson: all the hard, unlovely facts of human selfishness and pettiness sugared over with suggestions of large, vague self-sacrifices and atonements, and, as a mental exercise, scattered phrases about the nature of women which I must confess to finding frequently incomprehensible. What does it mean when we are told that Iris has a pagan body and a Chislehurst mind? or when the teller of the tale notices that the heroine does not comment on a Florentine mask in his room, and remarks, "That was how I knew that for her everything was inevitable. That is an important thing to know about a woman, for you know then that you will never know where you are"? or "the mind of a woman who is coiled in love is like a temptation one wants to touch"? But with all this semi-smart, tormented writing and all the emotional tomfoolery, there is the really bold new acceptance of the sins of the flesh as venial and inessential as compared with the quality of the spirit. In a pitifully milk-and-barley-water, backboneless way, the writer is trying to say the same thing as the author of *Tom Jones* and, by making his hero a heroine, to emphasize (as *La Garçonne* had already emphasized in a less sentimental fashion) the twentieth century doctrine of the single standard of sex morality.

To the direct question, then, whether the engrossing interest in sex has exercised a pernicious influence on contemporary fiction, the intelligent modern will probably reply, No. It is true that a large section of the more conservative and elderly reading public regard it as merely offensive and deplorable, and that is an attitude with which it is impossible to argue. If a person finds no interest in a discussion of such problems and does not want to hear them discussed—making no distinction between the pornographic novel, which exploits the merely fleshly instincts of sex, just as a prostitute does, and the imaginative novel, which deals with its romance, its tragedy, its comedy, and its farce—there is no more to be said. After all, no one need read anything he doesn't want to. It is more to the point to ask whether the open-minded reader, who is not in the least ashamed of his natural interests, gains anything from such novels, and I do not see how it is possible to deny that he does. One great appeal of the novel is its illustration of the intimate mysteries of the human heart, its exploration of all the pathways of human experience, its illumination of obscure places in our own consciousness and in that of others. Any novelist who can make us feel his creations to be human beings we all know, engaged in obscure struggles latent in the life we all know, is an interesting novelist. Sex is an essential part of the life of every normal man and woman, and creations of its infinite variety of influences, and comments on its infinite aspects and subtleties, are of interest to every normal man and woman. Our social morals may need washing, but they certainly don't need whitewashing. With so much accepted, the question becomes at once a literary one. Why do we enjoy some novels dealing with sexual questions and dislike others? Those who dislike what has been called the Freudian School of fiction, do so, I believe, because they find it both unintelligent and inartistic. Psycho-analysis having made a pseudo-scientific matter of what most observant persons had already noticed for themselves—that much of human unhappiness and ill-health was due to sexual inhibitions and repressions—it seems as if some writers were unable to see life in any other terms than those of psycho-analytical jargon. They may not use the jargon at all, but it is nevertheless implicit in all they write. They accept the assumptions of their new religion as if they provided a thoroughly mapped and charted guide to the mysteries of human personality—or, to change the metaphor, seem to imagine that because they have labelled their specimens, they therefore know all there is to know about what is in the bottles. But they appear to forget that no one is just an illustration of a theory, like Savina Grove in *Cytherea*, or Marion in *The Judge*—or Miss Forly in *The Goat and Compasses*, or the girl in *Women in Love*—who only gets complete physical satisfaction when she bashes in her lover's head with a ball of lapis lazuli! It is true, that if we examine the older literature in the light of modern psychology we shall find older writers unconsciously dealing with special types of sexual perversions. Heathcliff, for instance, appears to be a sadist, but *Wuthering Heights* is certainly not a study of sadism: Hamlet, again, may have loved his mother extravagantly, but the play is not a study of the Oedipus complex. Such examples indeed only prove how very little Freudianism has added to literature, for they show that any imaginative and observant vision of life implies a knowledge of anything vital to human character which has been "discovered" by psycho-analysis.

The psycho-analysts and even the too, too solidly fleshly school of best sellers have, however, one admirable lesson for society. They both illustrate how dull life becomes if you narrow it to nothing but sex. There is a cartoon of Max Beerbohm called *English Fiction, Ancient and Modern,* which is to the point. The first picture represents *The hero trying to control a guilty passion* and represents a strong, silent Victorian hero and a crinolined and ringletted heroine coyly unaware of his plight, with the note "quite dramatic and interesting, this." The second is *The Hero, trying to muster up a guilty passion,* where the modern man is looking thoroughly bored in the company of the stalwart cave woman staring him in the face. The dramatic romance has gone and only dulness remains. It is not a kindly cartoon, but there is a basic human truth in it. Complete freedom in sexual matters leads to complete boredom. As one of Aldous Huxley's characters says:

"Too much light conversation about the Oedipus complex is taking the edge off love. . . . It is only by inventing rules about it, which can be broken, it is only by investing it with an almost superhuman importance that love can be made interesting." I think the last sentence should read "permanently interesting," but otherwise it is surely very true. And as it is true of life, so it is true of literature. The real criticism against the psychological sex novel for the intelligent reader, is that it is a dull novel; "dull in a new way, so people think it great," as Johnson said of Gray. James Joyce has produced a unique human document in *Ulysses,* and no doubt it is a true human document and for the scientific student of psychology a very vital document, but from the literary point of view it is an uninteresting human document. The general impression left is a pathological, not a human, one. Norman Douglas declares that when a mature person reads an indecent book he either yawns or laughs, and there can be no doubt which of the two actions *Ulysses* induces. The pleasures of looking through the keyhole are the pleasures of immaturity, and the physical aspects of sex, whether they are reported directly or through the medium of associations they arouse in the subconscious, can never have any literary appeal except the very limited one of being "forbidden fruit." The perennial interest of sex, to the student of human nature, is its supreme importance in the whole scheme of life, and it must be shown in relation to the whole of life to be absorbing. There is no reason why a life in which sexual relationships are merely promiscuous need be uninteresting, but it is impossible for the sexual relationships in it to be absorbingly interesting except as comedy or satire. If sex is to be the subject of a serious piece of literature, it has to be shown as something far beyond a mere physical function, something which involves the whole nature of a man or a woman. I do not know why this is so, but the course of literature proves it. Mere promiscuity cannot be made serious and convincing; dignity and idealism remain absolutely essential to any representation of overwhelming sexual feeling, because somehow or other serious literature is always concerned with human loyalties, and though true love may be represented as unlawful love, it is never lawless love. You can have the triumph of true love as in *Jane Eyre* or in the Joe and Elsie episode in *Riceyman Steps,* or the tragedy of true love as in *The Mill on the Floss* or *The Constant Nymph,* or the tragedy of false love as in *Tess of the D'Urbervilles* or *The Three Sisters;* but you can't have any of the quality of triumph or tragedy in obviously light loves, like those of Ursula Trent or Mrs. Viveash.

This does not mean, needless to say, that sex cannot be treated in literature except in this manner of high seriousness, it only means that if it is to be shown as overwhelmingly important in life it has to be treated with seriousness to be successful as literature. It must also be treated with tremendous vitality of imagination.

Otherwise it simply becomes sentimental romance with the triumphs and tragedies of *If Winter Comes, Three Weeks,* and *The Green Hat.*

The trend of the modern treatment of sex in what we may call the intelligent novel is away from the straightforward romantic treatment, where the way between the Scylla of banality and the Charybdis of the unreal is so hard to steer, and the most interesting achievement of the new freedom towards such matters to-day seems to me to be in the spheres of comedy, irony and satire. Having escaped the old inhibitions and the old imposition of the romantic tradition as immutable law, the imagination of the contemporary writer can see the subject with an infinitely clearer mind. It is not possible to find out the truth about sex, or anything else, if you are not allowed to examine its facts and to discuss it openly and freely. Once the ban of silence is removed, by degrees clarity and reality appear. The modern writer is now free to interpret and represent the relationships existing between men and women and the immensely complicated and various impulses, actions and emotions which spring from the instincts of sex, exactly as they honestly appear to his human and intellectual observation. He has no need to create within the cramping limits of a moral code which requires heroes and heroines to follow certain standardized rules of conduct. It is perhaps natural that the result of the new freedom of outlook and

expression should be a gradual extension of the subject
from the sphere of an overwhelming seriousness to one
of irony and satire. The youth of a movement, like
the youth of an individual, is apt to show a certain unflinching earnestness, an eager solemnity, an insistence
on taking itself seriously, which gives way only later to
a capacity for a more detached view, with its implication of disillusion and experience. Each in his own
way, Zola, Ibsen, Meredith, and Hardy shocked public
opinion by enlightening it harshly as to the real emotional nature of men—and still more, of women. In
the same tradition we have, in the present day, the in-
tensities of D. H. Lawrence, the profound psychological
insight of L. H. Myers in *The Orissers,* or the sincere
and patient analysis of Virginia Woolf's *Night and
Day.* But Bernard Shaw created, or perhaps one
should say resuscitated, the satiric and ironic attitude
towards the realities of men—and still more, of women
—and from this attitude of disillusion has come what is
even more characteristic of contemporary consciousness. There is the rich, urbane, polished irony of
J. B. Cabell, perhaps the most wise as well as the most
witty of modern creators of eternal types, combining
in his satire the profundities as well as the frivolities
of all sexual relationships: emphasizing finally the truth
of that "cordial common faith" we all have that somehow love *is* very important in this "wasteful and in-
equitable process of living."

So at the last, with much excitement and breath and valuable time quite wasted, we find that the end of all is death. Then would it have been more shrewd, dear ladies, to have avoided love? To the contrary, we were unspeakably wise, to indulge the high-hearted insanity that love induced; since love alone can lend young people rapture, however transiently, in a world where the result of every human endeavour is transient, and the end of all is death.

We find the same polished irony, without the same warmth of sympathy, in Norman Douglas; or again, there is the sophisticated, cruel, almost despairing irony of Aldous Huxley, incapable of finding any manifestation of sexual passion which is not either a mere pastime to a man, or a definite obstruction in the path of his mental and spiritual development; or the whimsical humorous irony of *Serena Blandish* or of Stella Benson in *The Poor Man,* with the shrewd pungency underlying its charm; the radiant sanity of Rose Macaulay in *Dangerous Ages,* or the painful, gnawing irony of C. H. B. Kitchin's *Streamers Waving,* an extraordinarily brilliantly presented satire of one facet of modern life. It is the study of one of the million and a half "superfluous women" of England: an intelligent, neurotic girl, lacking in any real vitality of mind or character, who shares a Bloomsbury flat with two other young women, and has just enough money to make any occupation unnecessary. The story tells of a few summer months while she is in love with a commonplace, colourless young man; of her half-hearted and unsuccessful efforts to attract him seriously, her futile struggles, and her equally futile death. A tragedy without either dignity or meaning, an impressionistic sketch of one of the thousands of women with idle heads and hands and busy hearts, who drift impotently from deed to deed, and day to-day, the helpless sport of stray circumstance and stray emotion.

All these are significant types of the post-war treatment of sex themes, and the extension of humour and satire to the subject of sex is the most encouraging symptom in the contemporary novel, and illustrates, I think, a certain proportion of view which may come out of the mass of psychological, sociological, pathological, and emotional studies on this theme. It is the result to be hoped for from an attitude of frank acceptance of the facts of sex and a capacity to face all facts and all inquiry with dispassionate interest, free from prejudice and disgust and puritan intolerance on the one hand, and free also from the logical reaction from those attitudes, overemphasis of, and overabsorption in topics startling only because expression of them had been artificially restrained. One of the most important questions in a serious novelist's work is whether his vision adds width to a harmonized, balanced view of human existence, or whether it really narrows it by emphasizing only some one new aspect of life, of which he has become suddenly and extravagantly conscious. Many of the earlier writers on sex themes have only done the latter, and it has brought the sex novel into disrepute. Much of the criticism of it is, of course, merely the unconquerable bias of the older generation towards the old rigid standards of sexual morality, and in favour of reticence on all directly sexual topics; the attitude expressed by the story of the lady in the lending library, picking up a book and asking, "You are certain there is no Sex in this?" and being reassured by the reply, "Oh, yes, madam, I assure you it is only a love story!" But besides this frame of mind, there has often been a heavy pomposity of outspokenness which has quite as little proportion of outlook as had Victorian reserve. Wells is a bad offender in this way, D. H. Lawrence, during one phase of his development, and May Sinclair, when her imagination droops, as it unfortunately sometimes does through entire books. But this is not the general effect left on the mind from a comprehensive survey of the whole contemporary novel. The general effect is of an immensely widened view of the realities of human relationships and the intricacies and subtleties of problems woven about the natures of men and women; of patient, sincere representations of individual experience and observation; of a passionate sympathy with the struggles and frustrations and blunders of human beings in the grip of the deepest of human instincts. The hope for the future, in literature as in society, is surely that the final outcome may be more of that sane, full-blooded, generous, humorous outlook we have had in the past in Chaucer and Fielding, the outlook approached nearer to-day by

Cabell than by any English writer, though much of it is implied though not directly expressed in the work of Arnold Bennett. It is the outlook of a frank acceptance of the instinct of sex in all its manifestations. An acceptance of it as the ecstatic pinnacle of fleeting human happiness, the source of rapture involving the body, mind and spirit of mankind and of womankind; an acceptance of it as no less the secret of furtive, hidden warpings and twistings and obliquities of the human consciousness; the spring of manifold grandeurs of sacrifice and steadfastness, of glories of faith, of splendours of the soul; the cause, too, of manifold cruelties, of manifold pettiness and meanness, vanities, and jealousies of the human heart; and, of far more importance than anything else, the foundation for amiable pleasure, sweetness, contentment, good will, harmony, liveliness, stimulus, comfort, and cheerfulness between simple men and women.

"The New Psychology"

"The New Psychology"

You would seem to know my stops; you would pluck out the heart of my mystery; you would sound me from my lowest note to the top of my compass; and there is much music, excellent voice, in this little organ; yet cannot you make it speak.   —*Hamlet*

Sown in space like one among a handful of seeds in a suburban garden, the earth exists; a revolving, tepid sphere, whose every rotation brings it relentlessly nearer to the moon's dim, white, rotten desolation. Dwelling in this spinning island of terror, under immutable sentence of death, is Man, who, whether we regard him with the Psalmist as a little lower than the angels, or as "an ape, reft of his tail and grown rusty at climbing"; whether we see him shouting exultantly that he is the captain of his soul, or meeting his fate with all the lumbering discomfort of a cow being hustled into a railway truck, remains yet the ultimate mystery.

The present age is unique in its evolution of a new method of approach to this mystery, and much of the fiction of the present day attempts an elucidation of the eternal riddle of man's spirit by the help of what we have somewhat bumptiously christened The New Psychology. It has become the fashion nowadays to speak as if in the present day we had discovered infallible means of understanding human nature quite unknown to our ancestors. Robert Graves, for instance, in a recent volume of essays, states: "There are new analytic methods which criticism never had at its disposal before to reinforce the merely emotional comprehension"—as if no former age had ever used its brains or faculty for observation at all! Constantly we find it taken for granted that mankind to-day automatically possesses knowledge and perceptions of himself denied to former ages. It is true that the average person gives more energy nowadays to an examination of Sex than of the Soul, to a discussion of Glands than of God, but it is difficult to see how, beyond an extended knowledge of pathological detail—with which literature has very little direct concern—we are thereby better fitted to judge human character and conduct than were Socrates, Shakespeare, and Balzac. It may be that science will finally explain man in quite other terms: we may soon be debating the question suggested in Samuel Butler's *Erewhon*, whether every sensation is not chemical or mechanical in its operation, "whether there is now a molecular action of thought whence a dynamic theory of the passions shall be reducible. Whether, strictly speaking, we should not ask what kind of levers a man is made of rather than what is his temperament." Then we shall have physico-chemical fiction instead of pathologico-psychological as at present, but presumably the novelists will still be trying to explain, in yet another way, the actions and characters, emotions and experiences which were as common to the Chaldeans of five thousand years ago, as to the inhabitants of Chicago to-day.

But though, to the reader ignorant of all scientific psychology, it seems as if the modern psychological novelist reveals very little, if anything, new about the human spirit, there is no doubt that the subject of the individual has been made a topic of literary study and report in a way which has never before been attempted. What was previously only known to the honest consciousness by private introspection and self-examination, has become the subject matter of innumerable novels. To realize something of the change in literary ideals we have only to consider for a moment the literary creed of the polite world of a hundred and fifty years ago.

I hold it very indecent [says Shaftesbury] to publish reflections, meditations and solitary thoughts. These are the froth and scum of writing, which should be unburdened in private and consigned to oblivion before the writer comes before the world as good company.

I fear the Romantic Revival must be held responsible for the egocentric novel: James Joyce, indeed, is the direct descendant of Rousseau, and though some of the moderns have intellectualized the romantic spirit, its central core remains untouched—the exploitation of self-consciousness for literary ends. And its latest

manifestation, the cult of the Unconscious, is not intellectual at all: it is a denial that the reason is the
instrument of progress and an effort to find the secret
of vitality beneath the horizons of the mind, in instances unrelated to mental processes: to minister to
minds both healthy and diseased by an examination of
that perilous stuff that weighs upon the solar plexus.
We are told that we can no longer delude ourselves in
the faith that the conscious will is the pivot of our
being. Consciousness is only like the visible part of an
iceberg, and we can know only an infinitesimal part of
our own nature. As D. H. Lawrence says in his *Credo*:
"My soul is a dark forest. My known self will never
be more than a little clearing in the forest. Gods,
strange gods, come forth from the forest into the clearing of my known self and then go back." In another
work he defines the Unconscious, saying that it is "that
essential, unique nature of every individual creature,
which is, by its very nature, unanalyzable, indefinable,
inconceivable. It cannot be conceived, it can only be
experienced in every single instance." This suggests
the Athanasian creed with its three incomprehensibles
being one incomprehensible, not by confusion of substance but by unity of person, and so on, and it is this
sense of dark mystery surrounding the whole subject
which makes the common-sense reader impatient of its
literature. Just as the sex symbolism of psycho-analysis appeals to those who have rejected the old religious
dogmas but who yet feel the necessity for some sort of

formula in their beliefs, so it seems as if the theory of the Unconscious appeals to those who have rejected the old religious superstitions, but who yet feel the necessity of being awed by a mystery. Now the instinct of all art is to bring order out of chaos, to impose form on being, and burrowing in the "unanalyzable, indefinable, inconceivable" is death to the artist. He simply gets lost there. This is very well illustrated in the person of D. H. Lawrence himself, whose beliefs seem to have brought his power of expression to a state of complete stultification. It is perfectly true that he is obviously passionately aware of something in human conscious-ness of which the average mortal is not aware, but it is something which at present, at any rate, he cannot ex-press completely in the terms of the art of fiction. It is an extension of sensibility from the consciousness of personality we all possess, to the consciousness of that hinterland of raw vitality from which personality springs, but although he can convey a sense of this raw vitality, and has a matchless power of describing pictorial environment, the fact that he has dispensed with all the study of character as the average person knows it, takes away all average human interest from his work. Fiction to us is still a creation of *vitality col-oured and outlined by personality*. In all Lawrence's later books, the reader's mind and imagination get blurred and befogged by a constant effort to follow ar-gument about what cannot be argued, statement about what cannot be stated, and by a constant reiteration of such words as "inchoate," "darkness," "apartness," "aloneness," "the living unutterable," "the forever unrevealed." Even when he does succeed in finding a symbol for the vitality he is trying to describe, as he does in the stallion St. Mawr, whose burning life seems to suggest "echoes of another, darker, more spacious, more dangerous, more splendid world than ours," we don't get any further. The rest of the story is merely silly, and we have no conviction whatever that the frustrated and despairing soul of the heroine will find anything more satisfying to her glands and ganglions in the isolation of a New Mexican ranch than she, or Mr. Lawrence, found in London or in a Sydney suburb.

It is clear then, I think, that this extreme Unconscious-egocentric position is almost a negation of artistic creation. Certain writers of the present have attempted through it to set up a new realm of literature in the underworld of being, to make the creation of novels almost a kind of "automatic writing," to give the subconscious a fountain pen and see what happens. The result has been a literature whose creators seem to be in a continual condition of tragic intensity, or torturing themselves to impart something which is only *just* audible to themselves, but which they feel convinced is of immense significance. They are confident that self-fulfilment will be attained by exploring the amorphous instincts latent in these hidden mysteries of being, but the result seems to prove that "self-expression" does not follow from the obvious course of sinking into self. It will be noticed, indeed, that the finest psychological fiction, that of Dostoievsky or Tchekov or Flaubert or, in English, a book such as *The Orissers,* or the work of Conrad, is never directly "self-expressive." The richness of the artist's own spirit is expressed by his insight into the general problems of mankind. All experiment, however, is interesting, whether successful or not, and the modern extension of the methods of science to literature, the patient exploration of the mysteries and intricacies of human personality is an adventure which pricks natural human curiosity. Moreover, it has already had amazing results. Henry James fashioned out of such curiosity nothing less than a whole philosophy of art, illustrating very clearly Bernard Shaw's definition of a great artist as one who adds a fresh extension of sense to the heritage of the race, giving his readers a new intenser sense of inner emotional realities, just as Shaw himself has given us a new intenser sense of human fact. The Russians again have taught us to appreciate the confusion and dislocations of the impulses of life in an entirely new way. Dostoievsky may seem to us a gigantic pathologist, analyzing a psychology largely unintelligible to English minds, but a book like *The Brothers Karamazov* must come to all as a revelation of the possibilities of narrative to elucidate human consciousness.

The chief experiments in English contemporary literature, beyond D. H. Lawrence's obsession with the unconscious, have been the efforts to capture the *immediate* in consciousness in the works of Dorothy Richardson and James Joyce. "Nothing can be expressed in words," says Miriam Henderson in *The Trap*, Dorothy Richardson's latest book, but she has, nevertheless, succeeded in expressing in words something which no one else has quite expressed. One may find it unimportant and uninteresting, irritating and irksome, but her originality of creation is undeniable. She is an impressionist: that is, she is entirely occupied with the reporting of the impressions made upon her conscious and unconscious mind by the experience of life. The experiences themselves are nothing; she tells no direct story, describes no character directly. Life to her is not a matter of incidents and human contacts, it is something eternally flowing behind all incident and all character, something always active, yet always masking itself to the world, the hidden, but true, essential personality of each individual soul. Remorselessly she drags that of one soul out into the light of art, and analyzes it. The method has many objections. For one thing there is no reason why subconscious life should be any more "true" or "essential" than conscious life: the ingredients of a pudding are no more true or essential than the pudding itself when it is cooked. Raw material is raw material, whether in art or life or cookery, and the subconscious activities of the mind of man must be present in some form in the conscious being he presents to the world, and therefore detectable by the observant. Again, the concern of Miss Richardson being entirely with the immediate in consciousness, the result must of necessity lack all proportion or perspective as a vision of anything beyond the immediate. Nothing can be seen except in relation to the moment at which it happens: whether Miriam refuses an offer of marriage, or has tea at her club or interviews the landlord, or listens to her roommate going to bed, makes no difference. Past and future are annihilated. There is no "composition" in her life; it simply flows on, always apparently at the same emotional level and pressure. It has the effect of making life extraordinarily small. Perhaps it is; but somehow it is much jollier if we feel it invested with some sort of grandeur. I know of nothing more depressing in literature than this passage on the idea of human mortality, which is suggested to Miriam's mind by listening to her companion undressing at night.

But those other sounds never varied. And spoke of death. That was the worst, that they filled the room with the sense of death and the end.

They cast a long shadow backward over the whole of life, mocking it.

They were all there collected in the quiet room. Centring in the imagined spectacle of the teeth waiting in their saucer for the morning . . . the slow removal of the many unlovely garments, the prolonged swishing and dripping of the dismal sponge. All heralding and leading at last to the dreadful numb rattle of vulcanite in the basin. . . .

One wants to drown the taste of it by some mighty sonorous passage on the same theme:

O eloquent, just and mighty Death . . . how hast thou drawn together all the far-stretched greatness, all the pride, cruelty and ambition of man, and covered it all over with these two narrow words *Hic Jacet*.

Besides this monotony of emotional effect, there is the further monotony of the continual presence of the teller of the tale. Her subconscious holds the reader like the Ancient Mariner's eye, and he cannot choose but be submerged in its workings, to the exclusion of all drama, all humour, and all objective sight of the rest of the universe.

But there are certain aspects of life which can be conveyed more vividly by this method than in any other way. Suggestions of associated memory, for instance (though Dorothy Richardson does not specialize in this nearly as much as Joyce), and suggestions of that undercurrent of personality which we all feel beneath, as we play our parts among others in the daily round and the common task. Again, what one might call the "bathroom reverie" comes to life very well. We all know that when the mind is not directly and purposefully occupied with conscious thought, as for example when soaking placidly in a hot bath, there is a stream of impressions constantly slipping soapily over and across it. Also that more often than not, we then act scenes as we would like them to be, rather than as they are likely to be in actuality. The best example in fiction is the reflections of Christina Pontifex, in *The Way of All Flesh*, on the subject of the future of herself and Theobald. This kind of day-dreaming, whenever and wherever it takes place, is most relentlessly exhibited in Miriam, but, needless to say, without any of Butler's ironic humour. In *Interim* she is in a boarding-house: a young Canadian arrives and comes into the dining-room where she is sitting. He looks at her, that is all, but Miriam immediately starts imagining to herself a possible course of events.

A haunting, familiar sense of unreality possessed her. Once more she was part of a novel; it was right, true like a book, for Dr. Heber to come in in defiance of every one, bringing his studies into the public room in order to sit down quietly opposite this fair young English girl. He saw her apparently gravely studious and felt he could "pursue his own studies" all the better for her presence. . . . Perhaps if he remained steadily like that in her life she could grow into some semblance of his steady, reverent observation. . . . It *was* glorious to have a real, simple homage coming from a man who was no simpleton, coming simple, strong and kindly from Canada to put you in a shrine. . . .

Later she goes for a walk.

The hushed happiness that had begun in the dining-room half an hour ago seized her again suddenly, sending her forward almost on tiptoe. It was securely there; the vista it opened growing in beauty as she walked . . . bearing within her in secret unfathomable abundance the gift of ideal old-English rose and white gracious adorable womanhood given her by Dr. Heber.

The recording of all these phenomena is a new experiment in literature, but Dorothy Richardson's originality of method appears positively commonplace beside that of James Joyce. Joyce apparently accepts the Freudian dogma that the activities of the subconscious mind are the true personality, and his book is mainly a creation of two individuals by working from that premise. He states in one section of it that Bloom represents the scientific and Dedalus the artistic temperament, but though Dedalus, as the author, obviously does stand as a certain type of artist, to call Bloom an incarnation of the scientific mind seems a little hard on science. His creation is a most brilliant piece of embodiment, and must, I suppose, be regarded as a justification of the new method employed. That base, vulgar, limited, entirely materialistic, low-bred, graceless, smutty consciousness is complete to the reader in every detail. The method, however, fails grievously in its effort to give outline and reality to Dedalus. The very fact of Bloom's limitations makes his subconscious easy to apprehend, but Dedalus is a very different type. Embittered, self-centred, sensitive, fanatical, suffering from a persecution mania and a great emotional shock, his personality is further complicated by vast reading, a prodigious memory and an incessant mental activity. When every aimless and fugitive impression, every half-formed thought, every half-formed phrase and even word of such a character is presented, it becomes merely unintelligible to the plain reader. Everything that Dedalus has done, or seen, or thought, or experienced, or noted, or read, or heard in his life throngs his unconscious mind, and only he himself can possibly bridge the gaps, follow the sequences, make sense of the associations and interpret the stenography of that crowded mentality. Joyce has his own answer to all our objections, literary, social, and moral, to his book, "A man of genius makes no mistakes, his errors are volitional and are the portals of discoveries"; but the plain reader feels a little inclined to retort with Johnson, "The purpose of a writer is to be read," and, in spite of Joyce's reiterated statements of his own genius, to nurse a continued distrust of any work as literature, which is so full of outrages on the normal instincts of humanity and on the normal use of grammar.

So much then for the experiments in the new cult of the subconscious. The whole movement can be traced, like most intellectual and emotional experiments of to-day, to the decay of conviction in the accepted truths of the past age, and the consequent effort to find some further basis for belief. There is a passage in the preface to H. L. Mencken's *In Defense of Women,* which seems to me extraordinarily characteristic of the present day:

The only thing I respect is intellectual honesty, of which, of course, intellectual courage is a necessary part. A Socialist who goes to jail for his opinions seems to me a much finer man than the judge who sends him there, though I disagree with all the ideas of the Socialist and agree with some of those of the judge. But though he is fine, the Socialist is nevertheless foolish, for he suffers for what is untrue. If I knew what *was* true, I'd probably be willing to sweat and strive for it, and maybe even to die for it to the tune of bugle-blasts. But so far I have not found it.

The cultivated consciousness of to-day is very much like this: like Jurgen, compact of weariness and apprehension, who found nowhere what he desired, nor knew what it was he desired, tormented always by the thought that his knowing or his not knowing was of no account to anybody. There is nothing beyond the actualities of current existence to be the standard of achievement to the average man, and the average man, having discarded the theory that the universe is "a mighty maze, but not without a plan," is left with nothing but the mighty maze. "Consider well your neighbour, what an imbecile he is," as Norman Douglas says, and everywhere we see youth torturing itself about its own and other people's futility; discerning the effort of life so incommensurable with the result; haunted not only, not even so much, by the pain, disease, sorrow and evil of the world, as filled with disgust of its stupidity, its paltriness, its vulgarity, its meanness. "A common greyness silvers everything." In medieval times there was a human failing, christened "accidie," which was the eighth deadly sin. It was that "tedium cordis" which "maketh a man hevy, thogtful, and wrawe. . . . It forsloweth and forsluggeth," and finally produces despair through paralysis of the will. I believe it is the same thing which the eighteenth century called the Spleen and perhaps it is the same thing as the disillusion of to-day.

However that may be, the literary impulse, finding itself balked in its old activity of glorifying the triumphs of a universal moral scheme, has shifted its aim. General truth being so unsatisfactory, the alternative is individual judgment. We have already seen, in an earlier chapter, how the most significant work in the novel is along these lines, and it is the same impulse which is behind the modern fashion for autobiography. The present generation of intelligentsia have almost all experienced the loss of an old faith, a period of disillusionment, and have either found an abiding habitation there, or in some new faith born of individual experience. It is natural that these phases of human development, these frictions between the ego and the world, should be of engrossing interest to those who have suffered them, and that the creative impulse should fasten on to them for its use. Fielding says in the introduction to Book II of *Tom Jones*, "We have entitled this our work a history and not a life: nor an apology for a life as is more in fashion"; and we must own that apologies, or at least explanations, of lives are the prevailing fashion now. Since the publi-

cation of *The Way of All Flesh,* the father of the new
type of autobiographical novel, the problems of hered-
ity and environment, of the individual in conflict with
society, have been the most popular and powerful elements in English fiction. Life, pure and simple, is the
subject-matter, though perhaps those are not quite the
epithets to apply to the result. The present century
has seen the birth of what one critic has called "The
New Realism." This doctrine states:

It is enough that a thing should have happened for it to be
recorded, and that a sentiment should have been entertained
for it to be analyzed. Let the soul of the young man reveal
itself. It is precisely the hidden thoughts and secret sins
which make up the life of the character. Let them be faced
honestly just as they presented themselves.

"Look in thy heart and write!" in fact, and it is advice which both contemporary young men and young
women have not been slow to take advantage of. If
one happens to be what Mr. Polly calls "the skeptaceous sort" one may sometimes suspect whether the
young people have quite as many of the secret sins as
they lay claim to. Indeed, there is a certain type of
modern young Pharisee who seems to boast of being
not better but worse than he really is, a kind of sheep
in wolf's clothing. He stands in the temple of biographical fiction piously thanking God (or his
ganglions) that he is not as other men, quiet, home-
loving, kindly, reserved, but, on the contrary, has pub-

licly abolished the Deity, shaken off the tyranny of parents and avoided sex repression at all costs. It is perhaps natural that the new realism should produce a good deal of very raw egotism, that its practisers should be a good deal more interested in their own psychology and environment than in general human life; more anxious to illustrate facts about themselves than about general human nature. No one would deny the sincerity of the fiction produced by this ideal, but sincerity is not enough: the merit of meaning well is sometimes a difficult thing to forgive, in literature, as in life. As is inevitable, there is a great sameness of experience among the writers of biographical fiction. It is they who have created the dissection of family life in English literature, and since the publication of *The Way of All Flesh* every home is shown as a Heartbreak House. "My parents were gods till I was ten, masters till I was seventeen, and then they became nuisances," says a modern hero, and it is a good generalization for the heroes of this type of fiction. We see children tortured by lack of sympathy and understanding; their minds stunted and deformed by so-called education, their spirits warped or crushed by convention, prejudice, and superstition. When youth comes, it too is wretched, because, as Somerset Maugham says, young men "must discover for themselves that all they have read, and all that they have been told is lies, lies, lies, and each discovery is another nail driven into the body on the cross of life." And of course there is

Woman, and there are trivial lecheries to describe and a grand passion, and all the rapture and all the sick heavy obsession of love. And they must all find that they are seeking they know not what, and that they have moods in which they feel in tune with the rhythm of eternal forces, and fall back again into feebleness and the tyranny of the actual. This is the skeleton of all modern biographical novels that I have read, and whether that skeleton is clothed with living flesh and inspired with living spirit depends upon the genius of the writer. An autobiographical novel is like a bus that plies the same route whether it be empty or full. Such stories need not, of course, have the unity of design which a novel with a plot must achieve, for that is outside their scope. A plot has a course and a conclusion, but life only has a practical and arbitrary conclusion by death—as a quality and as a universal experience it does not conclude, it persists. Each individual personality, however, is something unique, and the quality of biographic fiction is in the vigour and vividness with which a personality is translated into the written word. The individual is constantly absorbing life and its multitudinous phenomena: there is always a kind of transubstantiation going on—incidents, relationships, emotions slowly producing the matured consciousness—and individual conduct is the fabric woven on the loom of time from the warp of circumstance and the woof of character. The test of the biographical novel, therefore, is the vitality of the central character, and whether everything that happens in the story happens so because of the individual way of thinking and feeling of that central character. If we feel the personality is simply constructed to fit a certain scheme of conduct, to give a certain meaning to experience, it inevitably fails, as Hugh Walpole's *Fortitude* fails or May Sinclair's *Harriet Frean*. The character must be created by its experience, as Ernest Pontifex is created, or Edwin Clayhanger. But besides this question of integrity of conception, there is the further question of the distinction of the accomplishment. Biographical novels can be most paralyzingly dull. What Henry James calls the "saturation" method of fiction has this great danger. We may become completely immersed in the consciousness the author is representing, but that immersion may produce either a glow or a chill. To produce the glow there must be something which brings that shock of *discovery* which is present in all fine literature, that magic alchemy which transforms the stuff of life into the stuff of art. But how often life proves stubborn: the lead remains as lumpish as ever, the gold will not come. J. D. Beresford tells us of Jacob Stahl, "There was some failing in the quality of his imagination, by which failing he fell short of anything approaching genius." Mr. Beresford would probably be the first to agree that he was criticizing his own talent here. The Jacob Stahl trilogy is a solid, honest, straightforward chronicle. The hero is a lovable character, so clear-sighted about himself, so unpretentious, so entirely without self-pity for his failures, and his creation is sincere and direct and convincing —but it is just a little heavy and monotonous. So, too, in spite of all its searching and painful reality is much of *Of Human Bondage,* and the same intermittent flatness is in *Mary Olivier* and *Young Felix* and *Arnold Waterlow.* There will be a fine, mellow, full-bodied flow of narrative for a while, and then it will taste as if it had been standing a long while with the cork out.

Sometimes again, there is an irritating lack of proportion in such novels. Of course the blunderings and questionings and idealisms of adolescence are very real and engrossing—to adolescence—but the interest to the mature mind is to see them in relation to some general view. We may recognize very clearly from bitter memories of our own pathetic youth, the kind of helpless, young, foolish, ignorant creatures, Michael Fane, and Mooncalf, and Felix, and Amory Blaine were, and as social documents no doubt such chronicles are of value; but it is always one of the disappointments of human limitations that one cannot at the same time join the procession *and* watch it from the window. Youth has to be detached from itself before it can see itself clearly. It is significant that in all these novels it is the childhood scenes which seem most perfectly created: Michael Fane and his sister in Kensington, Philip Carey's school days and the rectory at Blackstaple, Jacob Stahl's life in his aunt's cottage.

The fact that the novel is primarily a story of interest and entertainment to ordinary people, because it tells of ordinary people and their problems and activities, must make the straightforward biographical novel of far wider general appeal than any new experiment in psychological fiction. The average reader, who leads an average life, has an invincible instinct that the human spirit should be shown in action. Our conception of life may be entirely mistaken; beside the "wise passiveness" of the Chinese for example, our fretful preoccupation with the actual seems sometimes almost indescribably petty; but if we belong to a Western civilization we are born with certain traditions in us, of which we cannot rid ourselves. We may be like Nicholas in *The Orissers,* feeling that the true wealth of personality is elaborated within by concentration and meditation, and that the world of action and accident is a perpetual temptation to the dissipation of energies, to the avoidance of the ideal of Static Being. But we cannot escape the conviction that it is the business of our life to harmonize *all* the elements which it presents to us, to deal in some satisfying way with our inescapable though abject condition of earthliness: a condition which, however much we may resent it, is the very kernel of existence. We hold life on those terms, and it has got to be lived on those terms. From that standpoint we must regard it as a problem, as a spectacle, as an art. Jurgen would not possess Helen, who is perfection, for, he says:

"At the bottom of my heart I no longer desire perfection. For we who are tax-payers as well as immortal souls must live by politic evasions and formulæ and catchwords that fret away our lives as moths waste a garment: we fall insensibly to common sense as to a drug, and it dulls and kills in us whatsoever is rebellious and fine and unreasonable. . . . I am a creature of use and wont. I am the lackey of prudence and half measures, and I have put my dreams upon an allowance."

The fascination of psychological fiction, particularly now that its scope has been extended to include not only the presentation of man's practical and emotional experience, but the intentions and adventures of his spirit, now that it includes, so to speak, the technique of Rembrandt and of El Greco as portrait painters, is the fascination of watching, in the simplification and selection of life which art can, and indeed must, produce, the visions of reality which the imaginations of the writers of this age have created. What man,

> Dressed in a little brief authority,
> Most ignorant of what he's most assured,

sees as his being and his destiny. It is no very comforting discovery that any of the moderns make: no more comforting than life itself. It is the eternal platitude that the value of life is in the living of life. Philip Carey, the hero of *Of Human Bondage,* asks his friend, the failure Cronshaw, what he considers is the meaning of life. Cronshaw replies that life is worthless un-

less you yourself discover its meaning, and he sends
Philip a little piece of Persian carpet, saying that that
holds the secret. For years Philip keeps it, ignorant
of its significance, until he makes a discovery which at
last makes him happy, the discovery that life *has* no
meaning. That man is born, suffers, and dies; that he
serves no end by living and that it is immaterial
whether he is born or not born, whether he lives or
ceases to live.

The same uprush of fancy which had shown him with all
the force of mathematical demonstration that life had no
meaning, brought with it another idea; and that was why
Cronshaw, he imagined, had given him the Persian rug. As
the weaver elaborated his pattern for no end but the pleasure of his aesthetic sense, so might a man live his life, or if
one was forced to believe that his actions were outside his
choosing, so might a man look at his life, that it made a pattern. There was as little need to do this as there was use.
It was merely something he did for his own pleasure. Out
of the manifold events of his life, his deeds, his feelings, his
thoughts, he might make a design, regular, elaborate, complicated or beautiful; and though it might be no more than
an illusion that he had the power of selection, though it
might be no more than a fantastic legerdemain in which
appearances were interwoven with moonbeams, that did not
matter: it seemed, and so to him, it was. In the vast warp
of life, . . . with the background to his fancies that there
was no meaning and that nothing was important, a man
might get a personal satisfaction in selecting the various
strands that worked out the pattern. There was one pattern, the most obvious, perfect, and beautiful, in which a
man was born, grew to manhood, married, produced chil-

dren, toiled for his bread, and died; but there were others, intricate and wonderful, in which happiness did not enter and in which success was not attempted; and in them might be discovered a more troubling grace. . . . Philip thought that in throwing over the desire for happiness he was casting aside the last of his illusions. His life had seemed horrible when it was measured by its happiness, but now he seemed to gather strength as he realized that it might be measured by something else. Happiness mattered as little as pain. They came in, both of them, as all the other details of his life came in, to the elaboration of the design. He seemed for an instant to stand above the accidents of his existence, and he felt that they could not affect him again as they had done before. Whatever happened to him now would be one more motive to add to the complexity of the pattern, and when the end approached he would rejoice in its completion. It would be a work of art, and it would be none the less beautiful because he alone knew of its existence, and with his death it would at once cease to be.

Is There a "Feminine" Fiction?

Is There a "Feminine" Fiction?

Independence of spirit in young women is offensive and disgusting beyond all common offence.

—Jane Austen in *Mansfield Park*.

In *The New Monthly Magazine, and Universal Register* for March, 1820, there is an article entitled, "On the Female Literature of the Present Age." It opens thus:

There is no more delightful peculiarity of the literature of the present age than the worth·and the brilliancy of its female genius. The full development of the intellect and imagination of women is the triumph of modern times. . . . [In past ages] the contracted nature of their education—the tyrannical demeanor of the sterner sex towards them—and the yet more inflexible tyranny of custom, crushed the blossoms of their genius before they were half unfolded, or prevented them from diffusing their sweets beyond the limited circle of domestic life. . . . The gentle influences of feminine genius now shed over the whole literature of our country a delicate and tender bloom.

There is much more in the same style, where the writer expatiates on the grace and sweetness which the intermingling of female taste alone can bring to literature, since these qualities belong peculiarly to the female mind.

There is clearly no doubt in his reasoning as to the gifts which woman contributes to writing. Her work is "instinct with cheerful piety," she specializes in what Dr. Johnson calls "endearing elegance," her pen is as much a ministering angel as her personality.

I wonder what the author would say if he came upon the writings of Shaw or Mencken on the subject of the nature and mentality of woman, or could be let loose in a circulating library of modern fiction. His remarks do certainly bring home to the contemporary reader something of the revolution of the social code during the last hundred years. We might open a discussion of the modern novel with almost the same words as those of a hundred years ago, but how different the conclusion of the paragraph would have to be! There is no more marked peculiarity in present-day fiction than the worth and brilliancy of its female genius, but when the mind immediately seizes on the stern virility of a Sheila Kaye-Smith, the intellectual vigour of a May Sinclair, the aloof impersonality of a Willa Cather, the unsparing satire of a Rose Macaulay, or the pitiless analysis of a Rebecca West, we can hardly conclude that "the gentle influences of feminine genius shed a delicate and tender bloom" over the literature of to-day!

The question remains, though, whether there is anything in the writings of women which can be generalized about; whether feminine fiction is in any organic way different from masculine fiction; whether women really have a vision of the world and create a comment on the world which is as much their own as their especial physical characteristics. If they have, now is surely the time when it should show itself, for quite literally "the full development of the intellect and imagination of women" is possible now in a way it has never been before. Gone is the day of that delightful eighteenth century summarizer who snuffed the futile argument for women's education by remarking "their natural imbecility of mind renders them incapable of enlargement." Gone, too, Dr. Johnson's amazed comment on a woman speaking in public, "It is like a dog walking on its hind legs; it is not well done, but you are surprised that it should be done at all." Or again, the attitude of mind which made a contemporary reviewer of *Jane Eyre* declare that if the book were written by a woman it must be the work of one who had deservedly forfeited the society of her own sex; or the timid reliance on convention which made *Robert Elsmere* thrill the English-speaking world by its daring —these are almost, if not quite, unknown in the intelligent reading public of to-day. There is no knowledge of the facts of life or discussion of the truths of existence which is outside "woman's sphere," and even the theoretic arguments for admitting women into equal competition with men have now an old-fashioned ring about them. Miss Widgett, the suffragist in *Ann Veronica,* was so obsessed by the position of slavery and downtroddenness of her sex that she declared that when she thought of it she felt all over boot marks, —men's boots! But though as long as present economic and population conditions continue there must be rivalry between the sexes, the problem of adjustment is, I think, regarded as a practical and not a theoretic one, among the thinking section of modern society. It is not public opinion which any longer withholds a woman from any occupation or activity which may develop her intellect or her imagination.

Rose Macaulay in *Told by an Idiot* questions the fact that any new types of women are ever developed. Stanley Garden in 1879 is all for Women's Rights, social revolution, William Morris, and hand-wovenness in general; she represents, in fact, the New Girl. But Mrs. Garden is not convinced.

There shot into mamma's mind a question—had girls always been new? She remembered in her own youth the older people talking about the New Girl, the New Woman. Were girls and women really always newer than boys and men, or was it only that people noticed it more, and said more about it?

She concludes that there have always been the same types of girls, since there is nothing new under the sun, and indeed it is impossible to study types in the National Portrait Gallery and not to be convinced that women like Felicia Hemans or Mrs. Opie would easily have accepted modern criteria instead of their own and have written exactly like women of to-day if they had been born a hundred years later. Even if we imagine Jane Austen or Charlotte Brontë in our world we feel that although environment would have altered the course of their existences so vitally, it could do little to touch their essential personalities. The difference in women to-day and yesterday is not one of types but of frankness of view in the portrayal of types. Although the same kind of women must have existed in the Victorian world as nowadays, feminine fiction would not admit many of them as material for literature. There is a definite design in conduct which all Victorian heroines follow, though the pattern of their personalities varies according to the genius of their creators. But they all fall in love, have to pass through suffering and sacrifice, and win final happiness by patience and a devotion to "principle." Jane Eyre, Caroline Helstone, Anne Eliot, Fanny Price, Dorothea Casaubon—the curve of their fate is identical. If love can't find a way, the heroine must die, like Maggie Tulliver, while the slightest side step from virtue leads straight to disaster. Hetty Sorel must end as a convict and poor Mary Crawford has to be left unmated at the end of *Mansfield Park* merely because she holds the wrong point of view towards her brother's elopement with a married woman!

Compare all this with the varieties of fates among modern heroines. The only sameness is that they all fall in love, but the outcome of that incident is allowed all the variety it has in common life. Self-sacrifice is quite out of fashion now in heroines (unless it be to illustrate its fatuity or its pathological effects as discovered by psycho-analysis, as May Sinclair does in the characters of Eleanor Carteret, Mary Olivier, and Harriet Frean). The twentieth century heroine behaves exactly as she likes: she follows no code of definite conduct and her character alone leads her to her destiny. In *Dangerous Ages,* for instance, one young woman is left living happily with a married man, while another, having decided she wants a certain mate, goes straight for him in the most approved Ann Whitefield style—and gets him. (Both are represented sympathetically.) Stella Benson in *The Poor Man* leaves her beautiful heroine stranded in Peking, after an unsuccessful attempt to have an intrigue with a commonplace popular writer and detach him from his wife: all of which she narrates quite shamelessly to another young man in her hotel bedroom. Undine Spragg in *The Custom of the Country* tramples dignity and decency underfoot and is shown as getting precisely what she wants by those means. Ethel Sidgwick's *Laura* is not much better, while Willa Cather's *Lost Lady* ends, not like Becky Sharp, a disreputable demi-mondaine, but in an atmosphere of ease and respect. Anne Severn, just like Ann Veronica, Mary Olivier, and a host of others, never hesitates for a moment to become the mistress of the man she can't marry, and Clemence Dane and Hope Mirrlees give us careful and direct studies of Lesbians.

It is perhaps natural that it should be on the side of sexual relationship in youth that the new frankness is most obvious, but there is a very similar new outspokenness about the middle-aged woman. The Victorians made comedy figures of the weaknesses of the elderly, the Aunts in *The Mill on the Floss*, Mrs. Norris, Mrs. Bennett, Miss Bates, are satirized unmercifully. The stupidity and vulgarity and selfishness of comfortable middle-age were not spared, but never until the present day, I think, has there been a pitiless showing up of the "good" woman. There is a story of a man who replied to sympathy on account of his wife's death, "Yes, she was a good woman but somehow I never really *liked* her"; and that attitude is very apparent among our women novelists, though it was not a woman who first introduced it into fiction. Christina Pontifex in *The Way of All Flesh* was the first of that type, but Mrs. Potter in *Potterism*, Mrs. Fielding in *Anne Severn and the Fieldings*, and, better still, Mrs. Hilary in *Dangerous Ages* all have the same new note of malice, while E. M. Delafield has a perfect gallery of self-satisfied, sentimental, mulish middle-aged women, constantly causing direct harm to their fellow human beings by their selfish intellectual indolence and dishonesty. Muddle-headed, immature-minded maturity becomes part of the tragedy as well as of the comedy of life, and just as the serious unhappiness caused by the dull woman is a new note in feminine fiction, so in portraits like Miss Vivian in E. M. Delafield's *The War Workers,* Clare Hartill in Clemence Dane's *Regiment of Women,* and Anita Serle in *Legend* we find a novelty in women illustrating unflinchingly the hidden cruelty and greed of power in their own sex.

But though I have chosen examples entirely from the works of women novelists, there is nothing specially womanly or feminine in this new attitude to life. In all this, women are only following the general trend of the times. It is not woman's view as distinct from man's view: it is the general view shared alike by both sexes. it does show, however, that under modern codes of social ethics woman is free. She has complete liberty of action to develop her personality as she will (thwarted only by practical economic considerations) and complete liberty of speech to show the truth of existence as it appears to her, without blinking any facts or upholding any hypocrisies. Now, if ever, should feminine literary genius have real opportunity to flourish, and to embody in its art its own most characteristic and peculiar criticism of the world we live in.

There is, moreover, one very good reason why it is in the art of fiction that women should preëminently excel. It is a reason absolutely inherent in the nature of woman. Rebecca West, in *The Judge,* makes Marion declare that women are entirely dependent on their personal relationships for their happiness in the world. The heroine of another fine modern novel, *Jane, Our Stranger,* affirms the same: "I am a woman. My life is a long, strong, twisted rope, made up of a number of human relationships, nothing more." Now this generalization as to the nature of woman, which, to my mind, is the all-important generalization on that vexed subject, has a real bearing on the question of women and literature. The novel is the only literary form in which women can, with any sort of justice, be said to have reached the front rank of artists. Why is that? Surely because the scope and function of the novel is primarily to portray just that structure of personal relationships into which woman's whole being is built. There are exceptions, there is Emily Brontë for one, but in general woman succeeds as a novelist, because in that form she can bring her artistic vision to the creation of those problems of human environment which are the engrossing problem to the average feminine mind. For example, it would be altogether startling if *The Brothers Karamazov* or *Lord Jim* or *Tono Bungay*—or, to be completely contemporary, *Those Barren Leaves* or *Arrowsmith*—had been written by women: books in which first and foremost man recognizes the supreme necessity, either of finding some harmony between a conception of the universe and his own unconquerable soul, if he is to attain any complete and satisfying outlook on life: or of following an inner compulsion to do with his life what he instinctively and stubbornly feels he must do with it, regardless of social or human considerations. Even in the very rare cases where women have been able to give artistic expression to either of these truths about the nature of man (as Sheila Kaye-Smith does in *Green Apple Harvest* or Margaret Kennedy in *The Constant Nymph*) they do not suggest that they are ever feminine attitudes. I know no single woman in fiction who can stand as an example of one who finds a life based on ideas or an intense creative energy an essential factor in her happiness. The normal woman does not trouble much about relating herself to the universe; her problem is far more practical. She may, and very often does, make an entirely emotional matter of it, but it is the problem of how to harmonize her existence through her personal surroundings. These may be home, husband, children, family, friends or associates in occupation, but her problem is always, first of all, her human environment.

We find this truth illustrated over and over again in the novels of women, not only in those popular romantic works of fiction, where the truth is sentimentalized out of all actuality, but where we should expect less to find it emphasized; in the novels of the most impersonal, sexless, and ironic of our women writers. In Edith Wharton's *House of Mirth,* when Lily Bart had visited Nettie Struther's poor little home and family, she suddenly realizes for the first time her own impoverished life, and that it is not really money she needs, but a sense of human interdependence.

She had a sense . . . of an inner destitution compared to which outward conditions dwindled into insignificance. . . . It was the clutch of solitude at her heart, the sense of being swept like a stray uprooted growth down the heedless current of the years. That was the feeling which possessed her now—the feeling of being something rootless and ephemeral, mere spindrift of the whirling surface of existence, without anything to which the poor little tentacles of self could cling before the awful flood submerged them.

Nan Hilary in Rose Macaulay's *Dangerous Ages,* a much more modern type of young woman, finds her mind searching for just the same image as she reviews her own vague dissatisfaction.

Queer, fantastic, most lovely life!   Sordid, squalid, grotesque life, bitter as black tea, sour as stale wine!   Gloriously funny, brilliant as a flower bed, . . . unsteady as a swing-boat, silly as a drunkard's dream, tragic as a poem by Masefield. . . . To have one's corner of it . . . —what more did one want?   Human adventures, intellectual adventures, success, even a little fame, men and women, jokes, laughter and love, dancing and a little drink, and the fields and mountains and seas beyond—what more did one want?
Roots!   That was the metaphor that had eluded Nan. To be rooted and grounded in life, like a tree.

Or take that very interesting book, published last year, *Jane, Our Stranger,* by Mary Borden, one of those books which bring the pleasurable thrill of having faculties and emotions stirred and stimulated by an alert, sympathetic, and completely honest mind. The test of literature is, I suppose, whether we ourselves live more intensely for the reading of it: whether it quickens and vitalizes those emotions and mental faculties, so easily staled by custom and filmed by familiarity, by which we apprehend what we can of this experience we call life. This book does that. It is a study of an American woman dashing herself to pieces against the French society into which she is married by her mother. She stands for all that is finest in womanhood: truth, loyalty, tenderness of heart, but in the clash of civilizations she fails utterly because she cannot adjust her ideals into any harmony with the human beings she must live among. Ideals alone are useless to her, unless she can weave them into bonds of kinship with those nearest to her.

It is a book which illustrates very well the double point that woman depends on her human environment, and that her chief success in fiction centres in the portrayal of that environment. Her creation of it is far more wide and varied to-day than it was in the Victorian novel. Her range of problem, incident, situation and character is multiplied and diversified enormously: her handling of her material has a freedom and frankness hitherto unknown. But the field remains the same, although its boundaries have been so much enlarged, and wherever we find first-rate work among the women novelists of to-day, it seems to me that we find it in a study of intimate personal problems, just as we find it in the Victorians in a study of such problems. Rose Macaulay, who has a taste on the

mental palate like fresh celery on the physical, fails
when she turns from direct social satire, and tries, in
Told by an Idiot, to suggest the sweep of time and the
generations. She cannot compare with Bennett or Wells
or Galsworthy in the treatment of that theme. May
Sinclair fails as an artist every time she tries to blend
human interest with a discussion of abstract thought.
Sheila Kaye-Smith is really the only exception to the
generalization, and even if one suffers from a rooted
prejudice against dialect novels and people who are unaccountable this and middlin' that, who get in a vrother
and make a terrification, it is nevertheless impossible
not to feel the force and vigour of her work, the sense
of something beyond human strength which she feels
dwelling in the fastness of the earth, and the energy
and vitality of the character that springs from it. But
she is the only notable exception. Romer Wilson gave
promise of something altogether unusual in a woman's
writing in *Martin Schuler* and *The Death of Society,*
but that promise has not at present been fulfilled, and
if we think of the masterpieces of modern feminine fiction it is, I suggest, always of brilliant comedies, or
tragedies, of manners. We think of creations of atmosphere such as that surrounding *A Lost Lady;* of
the families in *Dangerous Ages* or *Potterism;* of the
domestic scenes in *Hatchways;* the vicarage in *The
Three Sisters* or that very different one in *The Cure of
Souls;* the girls' school in *Regiment of Women;* the
Edinburgh scenes in *The Judge;* the French and Eng-

lish domestic interiors in *The Little French Girl,* or any of those pictures from Katherine Mansfield which almost make the senses ache with the illusion of actuality.

There is distinction in all these books and brilliance in some, but when all is said, and in spite of the feminists with the queen bee in their bonnets, the fact remains that the creative genius of woman remains narrower than that of man, even in the novel. Just as, though Jane Austen is supreme in her own line, she is not as great as Fielding, so although Willa Cather is supreme in her own line, she is not as great as Conrad —or half a dozen men's names that might follow. In spite of equal education and equal opportunity, the *scope* of woman remains still smaller than the scope of man. There is a Sheila Kaye-Smith just as there is a Florence Nightingale, but the eternal platitude seems the eternal truism that, just as it is still in her close personal relationships that woman most naturally uses her human genius and her artistry in life, so it is still in the portrayal of those relationships that she perfects her most characteristic genius in writing.

Yokel Colour

Yokel Colour

I cannot abide to be in the country, like a wild beast in the wilderness.

—John Dryden in *The Wild Gallant*

There are as many ways of looking at the country as there are of looking at the town. There is the Docile fashion presented by an abler pen than mine in the following description.

The farm was wrapped in deep repose. Beyond the drowsy garden, which lay asleep in the afternoon sun, the fields lay in the afternoon sun, asleep: and still beyond, sleeping in the sun, lay the meadows. Beyond this lay the sun, asleep on the calm bosom of the sleeping pasture. Here lay the cows and kine, asleep in the shade of the drowsy trees, while the cattle slept in the shadows of the umbrageous foliage, and the blades of grass bent drowsily in the heavy somnolence of the hour.

At the other extreme there is the Unflinching fashion recently popularized by Mr. T. F. Powys, which is something like this:

WINSOME WESSEX or MR. BLASTER'S HOGS

In the road a small boy was torturing a frog; behind the hedge a tramp was raping a fainting girl; in the field an old woman was being gored by a bull, while the farmer enjoyed

119

the joke hugely from the window of his house. . . . In the Rectory the rector's wife was making jam and the rector appeared to be preparing his Sunday sermon. Though outwardly a bland, slow-witted but kindly man, inwardly he thought of nothing but money, food, and seducing young girls.

In the window of Mrs. Pansy's dingy house in the nearest seaport town there was a card, Lodgings: Special Terms for Seductions. Mrs. Pansy's chief joy in life was a young girl's ruin. Luckily the supply was enormous: they simply flocked to her lodgings to be ruined. One day the rector came down the street with his collar turned round, disguised as a seducer, and accompanied by the rectory housemaid. "This is the very place," he said, seeing the notice in the window. . . .

Alice was going to drown herself in the pond. A kind lady in a cottage took her in. She was one of the good characters, so of course the village hated her, and said she had murdered her brother and kept a brothel, and that made her have rather a wistful look. She already had the idiot son of the rector living with her and he and Alice fell in love with each other. But he was a good character, too, so the night before they were to be married, he met a tramp on the heath. "Who the bloody 'ell are you?" said the tramp jovially, and then he kicked him to death.

And Mr. Blaster just went on feeding his hogs. . . .

But apart from the Scenic novel, whose enumeration of rustic detail is inspired by the same spirit which loves to enumerate the detail of urban civilization, or any other minutiae, and apart from the Disillusioned novel, which is a passing literary fashion and belongs to what is generally called the Post-War temperament, there is enough fiction produced to-day with a definite background of the countryside, to lead us to the question of whether such literature adds to our imaginative experience anything which belongs to it alone—anything which we miss from the writers concerned with a more sophisticated psychology. It is obvious that it is quite possible to write of the countryside without suggesting any local or yokel colour at all. Jane Austen, for instance, creates characters whose occupations are those of people who live in substantial country houses but whose mental and emotional processes seem to owe nothing whatever to their surroundings: from their conversation and concerns they might just as well be in the town. And there are many novelists who portray the country life which only differs from town life by its society being poorer in numbers and in means of amusement, an existence which the eighteenth century dismissed as "supinely calm and dully innocent." Rose, the bourgeois town girl in E. M. Delafield's *Reversion to Type*, sums it up very well in her exasperated comment.

"Is living in the country in England always like this? I mean do you always potter about all day without doing anything, and look at the papers while you are waiting for the next meal, and take the dogs out for exercise, and never, never, never talk about anything but the rotten old garden,

and whether it rained in the night, and if the carriage can
go to meet the 4.30 train? Don't you ever, any of you, *do*
anything?"

This is the sort of life which Archibald Marshall creates very faithfully, the sort of life whose doom Galsworthy sees in *The Country House,* and Sheila Kaye-
Smith in *The End of the House of Alard;* the life of
the county squirarchy. It is being replaced rapidly by
a new race of dwellers in the country, who are in reality
townsfolk; people who use the country to play in and
to play with, but whose work and serious interests are
those of the town: the great multitude of summer resi-
dents and week-enders. The centre of gravity in English life has now quite definitely shifted to the towns,
and it is there that we find everything characteristically
"modern" in present-day civilization—industrial development, experiments in social reform, scientific in-
vestigation and all the "new" artistic coteries. Indeed,
many modern writers, of whom Mr. Powys is an extreme example, see in the life of the genuine country-
man and countrywoman of the present day nothing but
a degeneracy of physique, a narrow bigotry, and a poverty of mind and spirit altogether eclipsing their poverty of material possessions. That, for instance, is the
general impression left by *Bly Market,* part of a monu-
mental work called *Old England* by Bernard Gilbert,
which can hardly be criticized as a novel, but which
may be a social document of extraordinary value to future historians. It purports to give a "God's-eye view"

of a market day, and is a series of impressions, conversations, descriptions, and reports of mental processes dealing with and belonging to the inhabitants of
a country town and its surroundings. From it one
gains an overwhelming impression of the pettiness of
thought and outlook and character of the average rural
community: the petty business dealt with by the Guard-
ians, the petty legal transactions of the lawyer, the
petty offences before the Bench, the petty local considerations behind the political organizations, and the
Farmers Union: petty gossip, chaffering, grumbling,
dogmatizing, self-importance, wherever we are taken—
shops, schools, streets, houses, inns, banks, fair-ground,
tea-shop or church. It is an ugly, stupid, illiberal society.

On the other side are temperaments who feel as
Malory feels in Victoria Sackville-West's *Heritage.*

I have a great love for the country people; they are to me
like the oaks of the land, enduring and indigenous, beautiful with the beauty of strong deep-rooted things, without
intention of change. . . . I revere the simplicity of their traditional ideals. Above all, I envy them the balance and
stability of their lives.

And he thinks of the country as a vast cathedral teeming with worshippers, all passing in unison from ceremony to ceremony as the months revolve. Constance
Holme again, a little known writer of the Westmor-
land district, finds the "real things" in the life of the

farm, "trust in the morning and quiet in the evening, our own folk, and work and food and sleep—seedtime and harvest, cold and heat," while she sees the great gift of the country as "time to grow." There are few sensitive people indeed who do not have some perception of such truths; who do not have moods when that sense of continuity born of a familiarity with nature strengthens them emotionally, as it strengthens Mr. Sumption in Sheila Kaye-Smith's *Little England;* when they feel the mysterious romance of land—its wilfulness, its intimacy, its friendship, and its enmity; as Ishmael Ruan felt it in F. Tennyson Jesse's *Secret Bread;* and when they apprehend that welding of life and place which can make certain men and women seem almost a natural growth of a certain soil, as Joanna Godden seemed of the Rye Marshes. Few people, too, are without the sense of the beauty and the homeliness of the typical English farmhouse.

After the fashion of such houses, it stood back from a narrow lane: a low stone wall formed a kind of forecourt, which was filled with flowers, and a flagged path bordered with lavender lay stretched from the little swing gate to the door. . . . The steep tiled roofs, red-brown with age and gold-spattered with stonecrops, rose sharply up to the chimney stacks. You have seen it all a hundred times. Do you know how such houses crouch down into their hollow? So near, so near to the warm earth.

It is impossible, too, for the simple-hearted to miss the mood of Ishmael Ruan, when all his philosophy, all his changing beliefs in what was most worth while, resolve themselves into the passionate cry:

"Let Beauty not die for me. . . . May dawn and sunset, twilight and storm, hold their thrill to the last; may the young moon still cradle magic and the old moon image peace; may the wind never fail to blow freedom into my nostrils and the sunlight strike to my heart till I die."

And this sensitive spirit towards all sensuous beauty has given us such exquisite descriptions of the form, colour, and atmosphere of the English countryside as those of Walland Marsh in *Joanna Godden* and Boarzell Common in *Sussex Gorse* and the Cornish coastlands in *Secret Bread*, with a hundred finely touched scenes in the work of less known novelists. But mere keenness of observation and delicacy of descriptive skill are not enough in themselves to make a real "novel of the soil"; nor is the mere statement of elemental truths about the immutable earth and the essential reality of peasant life. These things have got to be felt with a passion which fuses character and background so indissolubly that the story cannot be thought of apart from the setting: it must be created from the earth, not constructed against a background of a certain locality, however carefully and even lovingly that background may have been observed and reported: it must have something of the quality which makes us conscious of the moors in every line of *Wuthering Heights*, though they are never directly described, something of the quality which makes it impossible to think of Tess, or Bathsheba Everdene, apart from Wessex. It is a quality which does not necessarily accompany what we generally mean by "brilliance," and which can elude a most gifted writer and yet appear in a quite minor one. For example, I miss it entirely in the work of Victoria Sackville-West. *Heritage* and *The Dragon in Shallow Waters* are both brilliant novels. They create unusual character and situation convincingly, handling personality and dramatic incident with force and sureness of touch. But although the countrysides they embody are most vividly pictured—presented with the most delicate ear for the cadence of language and the most acute eye for the apt image—somehow there is no interest in the setting: it has no emotional and human value, merely an intellectual one: it remains simply an adjunct to the story of certain human beings who are interesting quite apart from it altogether and who owe nothing to it. Again, in *The Pitiful Wife,* by Storm Jameson, the background of the Yorkshire moors, although it is so elaborately detailed, quite fails to produce the intensity it is meant to add to the tale, whereas in May Sinclair's *The Three Sisters* it is woven into the very texture of every emotional situation in the book. In the same way that marsh, "lying down on its face like a figure flung down to die," is an inseparable part of the fine grimness of Constance Holme's *The Splendid Fairing,* and there is a similar effect in *The Rector's Daughter,* by F. M. Mayor. There the countryside is but little intruded and its delusive simplicity matches both the art with which the story is told and the personality of the central character in it. It is the flat, uneventful, extraordinarily English countryside of Essex, but it is impossible to know that landscape and to read the book without being aware what Mr. Herbert felt in Mary Jocelyn, under her seeming meekness and apparent insipidity.

That depth and intensity of feeling, which rarely showed itself in her face, or even in her words. He could find it in his county's winds, which she relished in every part of her. When those winds came . . . then Mary came also. She seemed quite close to him, walking by his side again in the garden at Lanchester, where he first began to love her.

Most of all, however, we have this sense of the truth of human character which cannot be thought of apart from the soil it springs from in the work of Sheila Kaye-Smith. There are writers about the country whose genius burns sometimes with an intenser heat and a brighter light, but none which have such a clear and steady flame. Her general outlook is quiet, sane, generous and richly human, but she knows the passions which leave the mind bled of all thought, the heart bled of all feeling: she can create the aching misery of Dan Sheather in *The George and The Crown* when he has lost Belle Shackford, or the mystic intensity of Robert Fuller in *Green Apple Harvest,* or the agony of Mr. Sumption when he knows Jerry is dead, in *Little England,* as well as the tenderness of the love between Rose and Handshut or Robert and Bessy in *Sussex Gorse* or that between Joanna and the child Ellen in *Joanna Godden.* And unlike most writers about the countryside (and about most things in present-day fiction, alas) she has humour. She can show us the aesthete asking the tremendous old farmer, Reuben Backfield, if he has ever heard Pan's pipes; or show us Reuben himself asked to speak at a recruiting meeting, and replying by an address urging the Sussex farmers to stay at home and grow more grain; or Joanna Godden, in a burst of generous good will, giving (unasked) permission to the vicar to confirm all her farm hands. But her greatest artistic achievement has been in her creation of "the spirit of the land" in the characters of Reuben and Joanna. There *is* something epic and almost superhuman in the figure of Reuben, ruthless as the winds that blustered over Boarzell, hard as the stones that covered it, wiry as the gorse roots that twisted in its marl, dedicating his life to the purpose of owning the moor, "that great beast of power and mystery . . . strong, beautiful, desired, untamed," in the certainty that by craft, by strength, by toughness, man could fight the nature of a waste as well as of a beast: in that picture of him stopping his plough to shake his fist at the land on whose hard and sterile scab he is trying to grow grain: wading through blood and tears to his conquest of the soil: tearing women and the love of children out of his life as he

tears the gorse from his beloved land: battling with
seasons, elements, earth and nature, challenging God
and man to prevent him accomplishing his quest—and
finally triumphing.

And if *Sussex Gorse* is the epic of human hardihood,
of masculine single-mindedness, *Joanna Godden* is the
epic of woman's strength, of the stability and steadfastness of character which incarnates the vitality and sim-
pleness of the land itself. Joanna has no education
and no sophistication, she is tactless and bumptious,
she has a loud voice, a truculent manner, and a bar-
baric taste in dress, yet she remains one of the most
lovable personalities in modern fiction. She is "like a
plot of marsh earth, soft, rich, and alive," so healthy,
so vigorous, and with such glowing warmth and generosity of heart. We see her very well as she tries to
make friends with Martin Trevor at Romney market.

He would have passed on, but she barred the way, rather
an imposing figure in her bottle-green driving coat, with a
fur toque pressed down over the flying chestnut of her hair.
Her cheeks were not so much coloured as stained deep with
the sun and wind of Walland Marsh, and though it was
November, a mass of little freckles smudged and scattered
over her skin. It had not occurred to him before that she
was even a good-looking creature.

"I'm thinking, Mr. Trevor," she said deliberately, "that
you and me aren't liking each other as much as we should
ought."

"Really, Miss Godden, I don't see why you need say
that."

"Well, we don't like each other, do we? Leastways, you don't like me. Now you needn't gainsay me, for I know what you think. You think I was middling rude to Mr. Pratt in Pedlinge Street that day I first met you—and so I think myself, and I'm sorry, and Mr. Pratt knows it. He came around two weeks ago, to ask about Milly Pump, my chicken-gal, getting confirmed, and I told him I liked him and his ways so much that he could confirm the lot, gals and men—even old Stuppeny, who says he's been done already, but I say it don't matter, since he's so old it's sure to have worn off by this time."

Martin stared at her with his mouth open.

"So I say as I've done proper by Mr. Pratt," she continued, her voice rising to a husky flurry, "for I'll have to give 'em all a day off to get confirmed in, and that'll be a tedious affair for me. However, I don't grudge it, if it'll make things up between us, between you and me, I'm meaning."

"But I—I—that is, you've made a mistake—your behaviour to Mr. Pratt is no concern of mine."

He was getting terribly embarrassed—this dreadful woman, what would she say next? Unconsciously, yielding to a nervous habit, he took off his cap and violently rubbed his hair up the wrong way. The action somehow appealed to Joanna.

"But it is your concern, I reckon you've shown me plain that it is. I could see you were offended at the Farmers' Dinner."

A qualm of compunction smote Martin.

"You're showing me that *I've* been jolly rude."

"Well, I won't say you haven't," said Joanna affably. "Still, you've had reason. I reckon no one 'ud like me better for behaving rude to Mr. Pratt . . ."

"Oh, damn Mr. Pratt," cried Martin, completely losing

his head. "I tell you I don't care tuppence what you or any one else says or does to him."

"Then you should ought to care, Mr. Trevor," said Joanna, staidly, "not that I've any right to tell you, seeing as how I've behaved. But at least I gave him a harmonium first—it's only that I couldn't abide the fuss he made of his thanks. I like doing things for folks, but I can't stand their making fools of themselves and me over it."

Trevor had been miserably conscious that they were standing in the middle of the road, that Joanna was not inconspicuous, and if she had been, her voice would have made up for it. . . . He suddenly felt himself, not without justification, the chief spectacle of Romney market-day.

"Please don't think about it any more, Miss Godden," he said hurriedly. "I certainly should never presume to question anything you ever said or did to Mr. Pratt or anybody else. And if you'll excuse me, I must go on—I'm a farmer now, you know," with a ghastly attempt at a smile, "and I've plenty of business in the market."

"Reckon you have," said Joanna, her voice suddenly falling flat.

He snatched off his cap and left her standing in the middle of the street.

Then in contrast to her early stalwart good-heartedness and unquenchable belief in herself and the rightness of her standards, comes her own passionate experience and its distressful sequel, and Joanna "looking like a great, broken, golden sunflower in her despair," coming back to Ansdore to confess her folly to the superior Ellen, to renounce her beloved farm, to fall on her knees and pray:

"Oh please God forgive me. I know I have been wicked, but I'm unaccountable sorry. And I'm going through with it. Please help my child—don't let it get hurt for my fault. Help me to do my best and not grumble, seeing as it's all my own wickedness: and I'm sorry I broke the Ten Commandments."

And finally, nearly forty years old, to turn her back on the life and the heritage which have made her what she is: her lover, her sister, her farm, her home, her good name, all lost; but holding in her heart, as her dear fields held, the imperishable quality of solidity and endurance, a certain elemental and unshakable faithfulness.

The American Scene

The American Scene

He calleth trousers pants, whereas I call them trousers.
—SAMUEL BUTLER. *A Psalm of Montreal.*

FOR a person of one nationality to criticize the literature of another nationality is always a delicate under-
taking—more especially if it happens to be an English
person criticizing the American literature of to-day.
For there has been in the past, and indeed it is not unknown in the present, more than a hint of patronage
in the tone of English letters towards American letters,
and the writers of America feel, I think, and certainly
have just cause for feeling, a certain resentment of it.
It must be clear to any unprejudiced readers of the
critical journals of both countries that there is a very
definite inequality of critical justice on each side. In
so far as any generalization is true, it is true to say
that English critics still tend to be too harsh to American writers, while American critics still tend to be too
kind to English writers. The indifference of the cultivated English public to such an artist as Willa Cather,
and the acceptance of Archibald Marshall by the
American public as a modern Trollope, are single illustrations of this fact. The difficulty is that of traditional outlook. England finds it very hard to forget

that America is no longer English, and to realize that she has to be approached frankly as a foreign country, and her literature regarded with the critical detachment which would be accorded to the writers of France, Russia, or Japan. On the other hand, many of the leading critics in America, and a great part of the intelligent reading public, still have a rooted conviction that all the best books come from England, and obstinately persist in looking always down the arches of the years when English culture was the chief model to all intellectual America.

To criticize modern American fiction as if it were stimulated by exactly the same civilization as modern English fiction is absurd, yet it is inevitable that the Post-War outlook in all countries should have much in common, and that it should include many of the same conditions, whether it regards those conditions from a viewpoint, or from a point of view, whether it talks about a reaction to them, or their influence, whether we sense them from social contacts or judge them from environment. Contemporary American society and the contemporary American novel share the spirit of English society and the English novel in their prevailing atmosphere—the atmosphere of an all-pervading agnosticism. "I have been called a modern," says Sherwood Anderson, "and perhaps only deserve the title inasmuch as I am a born questioner." And the things questioned by serious American writers include all those questioned by serious English writers. First and foremost they question the creed of a moral law operating in the cosmos: the clear meaning of life accepted so simply by the late nineteenth century. At the end of Scott Fitzgerald's *This Side of Paradise*, the hero, Amory Blaine, makes the discovery that "Life is a damned muddle . . . a football game with every one offside and the referee gotten rid of, and every one claiming that the referee would have been on his side." Again, a character in *The Apple of the Eye*, by Glenway Wescott, suddenly finds that "the purpose of life is to go on, just to go on. . . ." As in England, this discovery has led writers to a more exact and minute examination of the actual facts of life as they appear to them to be, viewed independently of any dogmatic or ulterior significance, and they have been similarly led to a profound contempt for the representation of the facts of life in the work of their predecessors, and in the more popular writers of their own day. They examine and report faithfully on the realities of war, the relationships of the sexes, the ethics of Big Business, and so on: they lay bare the tragedy of Mark Twain and unmask the bitter cynicism of Jack London, as he confesses his own complete disillusionment in a letter and adds: "But I know better than to give the truth as I have seen it in my books. The bubbles of illusion, the pap of pretty lies are the true stuff of stories." Sherwood Anderson, in his creation of the figure of his father—that delicious blend of Mr. Micawber and Hjalmar Ekdal—and his account of the stories of his romantic past which his father would invent so blithely, illustrates very well the standards of sentimental and romantic unreality, the exaggeration of the nobility of negative self-sacrifice, of the ideals of the valour of men and the purity of women, whose dishonesty has so disgusted the present generation of intelligentsia. And in their disgust many of them have rushed to the no less dishonest position of the opposite extreme. Instead of taking life like eating cheese and enjoying the taste, they put it under a microscope and shudder at the sight; or spend their time, as Mr. P. G. Wodehouse says of one of his less happy characters, "going around searching for the leak in life's gas pipe with a lighted candle." This almost conscientious pessimism is the cause of a certain heavy air of self-consciousness which hangs over a good deal of the fiction by young writers—the atmosphere of Scott Fitzgerald, John Cournos, and Susan Glaspell, to name a few. The realization that most of the tenets impressed constantly upon their youth and adolescence have proved untenable when tested upon unsympathetic fact, has come with such a shock of disenchantment that they dismiss all "Victorian" beliefs as necessarily untrue—ending almost in the position of Cecil Graham in *Lady Windermere's Fan:* "When people agree with me, I always feel I must be wrong." Hence, too, the almost total lack of humour among the young writers of England and America, and their creation of such extraordinarily unpleasant people. There is a passage in Norman Douglas's *South Wind* where the Duchess declares that she doesn't like some character in a book, and Mr. Keith replies: "You have nothing but nice people around you, Duchess, why should you want to read about them? There is so much goodness in real life: do let us keep it out of our books. . . ." And the spirit of this agreeable banter seems to have become hardened into a deadly seriousness in only too many novels enshrining the despondencies of fledgling undergraduates and the tragedies of playboys of the Middle-Western world. The desire to get as much experience as possible out of life, without being bound by any of its responsibilities; the confusion of freedom from discipline with genuine liberty; the tiresome assurance that the young people of the present age are entirely different from the young people of any other age; the insistence on immediate problems to the exclusion of eternal problems; the glut of novels written for merely clever people by merely clever people—all these are both English and American. So, too, is the insistence on problems of sex, which sees the cities of America as "one vast juvenile intrigue," as Scott Fitzgerald does, which paints society as Ben Hecht does, or as R. W. Kauffman in *The Free Lovers,* which illustrates the caddishness of men, as in *Wings,* or the clingingness of women as in *Don Juan,* and which so emphasizes the pathology of the subject that in many novels we feel more inclined to speak of "the patient" than of the hero or the heroine.

Specially American, of course, is the presentation in fiction of local problems such as the treatment of coloured races or of the Jews, but the main revolt in cultivated America to-day seems a far wider one than is involved in any special piece of propaganda, or even than that which is presented by the changes in manners and morals which are the inevitable ebb and flow of the generations. Throughout the length and breadth of the continent, there is a profound and a growing dissatisfaction with the quality of the civilization which is now the typical civilization throughout the whole of America. England has no Sinclair Lewis, and although the human and social blemishes he so brilliantly emphasizes are present in English life and society—and indeed in *all* life and society, for Potterism is as wide as the civilized world—the *scale* on which they are apparent in the United States makes the problem incomparably more obvious and startling. It is the problem of the standardization of existence which has resulted from the mass production methods of America—the mass production of motor cars, victrolas, motion pictures, syndicated newspapers and standardized fiction in the popular magazines, and the still more deadly mass production of standardized education and a standardized measure of success. Sinclair Lewis sees it as Dulness made God: "a savorless people gulping tasteless food and sitting afterwards coatless and thoughtless in rocking-chairs prickly with inane decorations, listening to mechanical music, and saying mechanical

things about the excellence of Ford automobiles." This
is Main Street, but he sees Main Street as determining
the whole society of the country, "the greatest manu-
facturer is but a busier Sam Clark and all the rotund
senators and presidents are village lawyers and bankers
grown nine feet tall." In the same way there is little
difference between a small city and a large city; "the
only authentic difference between Nautilus and Zenith
is that in both cases all the streets look alike, but in
Nautilus they do not look alike for so many miles."
They are both cities which will have a Gladhand Week
and listen to a sermon on the Pep of St. Paul, inhabited
by thousands upon thousands of Babbitts and Picker-
baughs, all believing in the tenets of the Good Citizens
League, "all of them agreed that the working classes
must be kept in their place and all of them perceived
that American Democracy did not imply equality of
wealth, but did imply a wholesome sameness of thought,
dress, and vocabulary": men who meet you with a
greeting of, "Well, well, well, well," who are pious
motorists and cheerful Boosters, who think that any
demand for privacy is bad form, who live in an ecstasy
of honest self-appreciation: who christen a house
"Uneedarest," who think that sleeping porches and
swimming pools and a kind word in time will right the
wrongs of the world, who are convinced that culture is
an external asset, the result of a correspondence course
and a Five Foot Shelf of books and a Symphony Or-
chestra in the city: men who glorify energy merely for

itself and who worship bigness in everything—in scenery, in jewels, in muscles, wealth, or words: men who know the cost of everything and the value of nothing, and are all ironed out into a glossy mediocrity. These men are matched by the women: the narrow, gossiping busybodies of Main Street; Mrs. Babbitt, colourless, insipid, diligent, trying to find the Inner Key in the League of the Higher Illumination; or Mrs. Golden, with just enough aspiration to make her discontented and not enough to make her toil at the acquisition of knowledge and understanding. All, men and women, with physically mature bodies and childish minds as much alike as if they had been stamped out by an educative biscuit cutter.

There is, I think, no single thoughtful person in America to-day who is not conscious in some degree of these things and anxious to escape from them—from the antics of society climbers with aspirations towards the cosmopolitanism which great wealth can buy, to pathetic D.A.R. chapters clinging to European family trees and trying to pretend that America is really still as English as she was a hundred years ago; from any number of freak schools and colleges whose aim is to supply an education as unlike state education as possible—to a great deal of sane and well informed discussion. But we are concerned here with the influence of the prevailing form of civilization on the contemporary novel. The consciousness of that civilization seems to be the most powerful force in American fiction to-day, and the work of almost every serious writer seems to be either directly or indirectly influenced by it. The most obvious influence is naturally when the artist deals directly with the society around him as he sees it, as Sinclair Lewis does, or Upton Sinclair, or Theodore Dreiser, or Sherwood Anderson, or Edith Wharton. All these writers are in revolt against their material—all are filled with active hatred, or at least active dissatisfaction with the conditions of life they report, and this frame of mind towards their material inevitably affects their work. Now there is no reason why a work of art should not be inspired by hatred and contempt of certain social characteristics. There is Balzac, for example, who is concerned with little else. But that hatred burns so fiercely from the pages of *La Comédie Humaine* because it is presented with such intensity of vision into eternal types of human character as well as by such matchless skill in the presentation of relevant detail. Beside it, Upton Sinclair's savage bludgeoning appears ponderously crude and even Sinclair Lewis imprisoned stiffly within an attitude. "It is not individuals but institutions which are the enemies," he declares, but in his books this never appears clearly, hence the common, and semi-truthful criticism of his work that it is humanly unfair—that America is not merely a place where old age is sodden like Doc Vickerson or repulsive like the Widow Bogart or dishonest like Mr. Thompson; where middle age is self-satisfied, stupid, superficial, and hypocritical like the Tozers or the Babbitts; where youth is coarse, blasphemous, lazy, pretentious, greedy, bibulous, and rowdy. Sinclair Lewis's enemies—that is, about seven-eighths of the people who read him—overemphasize this point, but it is nevertheless true that, with the exception of the idealism of Martin Arrowsmith, he creates no positive standard of life in living human figures. His genius is in his creation of social atmosphere; the special flavour of a dinner party, or a meeting or a railroad journey; in his uncanny memory for the conversational inanities of half-baked minds and in his relish for revealing detail—his instant perception of how a chair was placed or what things were on a table, and the significance of these matters to his general theme. But his art remains essentially external: it is a mosaic of the actual, but of pieces of the actual which have been carefully chosen for a certain special purpose—to illustrate the pattern of the standardization of society, not the general rhythms of humanity: it is the mosaic of a tessellated bathroom, not of the floor of St. Mark's. Sinclair Lewis has none of that double vision which characterizes Arnold Bennett's creation of provincialism. He sees human beings very vividly from his own point of view but he cannot identify himself with people foreign to his own mind. He sees the poverty of life in Gopher Prairies or the Zenith Athletic Club, the hypocrisy of commercialized science, the hollowness of merely material ambitions—sees, too, the pathetic goodness which is in Babbitt or the bewilderments and

kindness and sturdy endurance of Doc Kennicott, but
it is all simply a faithful reproduction of his own direct
intellectual vision. Arnold Bennett would have shown
us what Bea, the Swedish maid, actually thought of it
all, and would have created a picture of Sam Clark's
own enjoyment when he was out hunting with the doc-
tor, or spending what to him seemed a jolly evening
with his friends. Sinclair Lewis's criticism of society
really has more in common with Wells's, but without
the fine positive enthusiasms of Wells, and he lacks too
the exquisite comedic detachment of Rose Macaulay's
social satire. His work is the brilliant indictment of an
evil by means of selected pieces of actuality which illustrate that evil, but his conception (except in *Babbitt*) is not realized intensely enough to express itself
entirely in the terms of that actuality. Instead of his
reported action and dialogue conveying completely his
satiric intent, he is forced to intrude far too much direct critical comment, every word of which mars his
books as works of art. For example, a passage like
this in *Arrowsmith*:

Gradually Martin's contemplation moved beyond Almus
Pickerbaugh to all leaders, of armies or empires, of universi-
ties or churches, and he saw that most of them were Picker-
baughs. He preached to himself, as Max Gottlieb had
once preached to him, the loyalty of dissent, the faith of
being very doubtful, the gospel of not bawling gospels, the
wisdom of admitting the probable ignorance of one's self and
of everybody else, and the energetic acceleration of a Movement for going very slow.

It is portentous, like the later Wells, and it is bad workmanship. A careful artist never formulates his philosophy or social criticism so directly: he makes it implicit in dialogue and incident, as it is in *Clayhanger* or in *Mr. Polly* or in *Dangerous Ages,* or as it is in a satire on Main Street and Nautilus just as biting as Sinclair Lewis's—Edith Wharton's *The Custom of the Country.* Here no satiric or ironic comment is made throughout, but satire and irony are packed into every situation in the development of the story, and the artistic forces of restraint, discipline, and discrimination add far more to the effect than any facile philosophizing—as they do too in the same author's indictment of New York society in *The House of Mirth,* where the whole subject is presented with a civilized suavity of touch rare enough in any of the English-speaking countries.

The same constructive weakness, the same personal instead of impersonal absorption in a theme is more apparent still in the novels of Theodore Dreiser, and indeed would make them completely unreadable if they did not illustrate a quality which Sinclair Lewis lacks almost entirely—an inexhaustible, patient curiosity about the mysterious mental and emotional processes of all kinds of human creatures. In his attempt to elucidate these processes, Dreiser uses a plodding simplicity of attack which at times reminds one of the style of *The Young Visiters:* "She was beautiful in a light purple walking costume of masterly design"; "She was extraordinarily artistic and delightful"; "Mrs. Finch's heart was practically broken." He will use extravagantly unreal and stilted dialogue, bathos and cliché are always at his pen's point; we are told that women are witty, but we never hear any wit; we are assured that they are charming, but we never feel a particle of their charm; he has no picturesque quality, no humour, no subtlety, no elegance—nothing but this ugly solidity of craftsmanship and a terrific determination to express somehow the forms of life and the forces of life which he has seen and felt with such intensity. We feel the same determination in Sherwood Anderson, though he writes from the standpoint of a much later consciousness—the specifically modern consciousness which is represented in England by D. H. Lawrence and James Joyce. He is a very lovable writer in his earlier, simpler style, but his later work is difficult to apprehend fully—perhaps especially for a foreigner. He seems to be struggling to give expression to a drama of inner realities which he feels behind the mechanistic civilization he lives in, and to be sensible that the usual methods of fiction are totally inadequate to interpret these human verities, but at present his work reminds one that an extension of sensibility has *in itself* no *literary* value. Like D. H. Lawrence, he seems to be struggling to say something for which at present he has not found the mode of expression: we feel the struggles, but do not catch the reality he wishes to interpret. It is impossible not to feel, however, that he may be a figure of great literary significance.

The effect of an environment to which they are definitely hostile is again behind the work of the novelists who seek an escape from it by the deliberate choice of alien themes. Cabell's sensitive if self-conscious irony invents the kingdom of Poictesme as his literary pleasance, Hergesheimer finds his most successful material in the romantic past of *The Three Black Pennys* or the coloured pictorial atmosphere of *Java Head*, and Stephen Benet wanders from an incredibly aristocratic South to passionate prostitution in Paris. Or again, there are the writers of the countryside. Here again, we find the same distinction which we have already suggested in the critics of industrial society, between what we might call constructed and created work. Ruth Suckow's *Country People*, for example, is parallel in spirit, though not of course in method of presentation, with *Main Street*. It is external. It gives a selection of facts to illustrate the dulness of people on a middle-western farm, people whose lives are as drab as their homes and as flat as their fields. It is a sincere deliberate protest against the ugliness and narrowness of such a life, but it remains a criticism of environment, not an interpretation of human experience: it describes the details of a certain way of life, but it does not convey the quality of that life beyond its externals. The same criticism applies to Edith Kelly's *Weeds*, patient and painstaking though that book is. Compare these books with *Maria Chapdelaine* or, nearer home, with the first episode in *The Apple of the Eye.* The other two episodes lack conviction, the author's imagination flags and becomes only visual; but in "Bad Han," it is alive and racing. "Beauty" is a vague critical term, but in the sense of illustrating the perfect use of artistic means to an artistic end this story is exquisitely beautiful. Background is there—suggested by a rare delicacy of observation and sensitiveness of description, and against that background is human cruelty and sweetness, weakness and strength, endurance, serenity, compromise, triviality—a myriad mood of the spirit of man and woman, welded together in the vitality of an authentic work of art. There are flashes of the same genuine creative power in *The Lake*, by Margaret Ashmun, and in *So Big*, with its suggestion of character that reflects the reality of the soil—a nature partaking of the wide spaces of the sky and the prairie, holding in its heart something of the fierce tenacity of frost, the warmth of spring sunshine, the rich blending of colours of the kindly fruits of the earth. But the masterpiece in this type of writing is Willa Cather's *My Antonia*. It has something of the epic quality of *Joanna Godden,* but more poetry—more of the significance of the eternal in the temporal, the universal in the particular. Just as Mr. Shimerda, kneeling before the Christmas tree in an alien land, is a living, pitiful old man and yet suggests and incarnates all the passionate nostalgia of every exile for his fatherland and his faith, his reaching out of impotent hands towards the memories of his lost youth and home and happiness, so the figure of Antonía herself, a living individual child and woman, incarnates and suggests also the hope, the fulness, the beauty, of all free, growing, fruitful things of the earth.

Deep down in her there was a kind of hearty joviality, a relish of life not over delicate, but very invigorating.

Or again:

She had only to stand in the orchard and put her hand on a little crab-tree and look up at the apples, to make you feel the goodness of planting and tending and harvesting at last.

There is something of the same spirit, of the same feeling about the warm vitality and hospitality of America, in *The Golden Village*, by Joseph Anthony. It is slighter, but the translation of the picaresque romance into modern terms is extraordinarily well done: it has the sharp tang of a real zest for life, and the direct and simple expression of the common emotions of common lives is alight with clear-cut humour and clear-cut pathos.

Finally, there are naturally individual works of art which can in no way illustrate the theme of what is peculiarly American in contemporary fiction. Books like *Ethan Frome*, which holds the still, grim, deep, dark beauty of a mountain tarn, or *A Lost Lady*, that exquisite study of a woman with her "many-coloured laugh" who wanted life on any terms, and who yet "had always the power of suggesting things far lovelier than herself, as the perfume of a single flower may call up the whole sweetness of spring." A story told with matchless subtlety and artistic economy. These are masterpieces whose scene happens to be laid in America and whose creators are Americans, but are not more closely linked than that with the problems of the modern American world. But in view of the artistic output in the field of fiction alone, it is difficult for a foreigner to grasp why the radical critics continue to insist that a man cannot be an artist in America—that its civilization crushes an artist out of existence. The way of the artist is not easy in any country—except the way of the flatulent Bohemian who plays at being an artist in the Quartier Latin or in Chelsea or in Greenwich Village, but the view that it is not only difficult but impossible in America is surely disproved by the world of modern American letters. There are, of course, still, and perhaps always will be, the American writers, like Edith Wharton or Anne Douglas Sedgwick or Elinor Wylie, who feel themselves more in sympathy with the European tradition and the European sophistication of outlook, but there are new American artists who have definitely accepted the truth that for them writing must be American writing, its vitality must be American vitality, its inspiration American life as they know it. They know that this new literature cannot aim at an imitation of European ideals, because it is not European, but that, whether the passion which is behind its creation is a passion of revolt from certain aspects of American civilization, or the passion of interest in and enjoyment of the common human lives of the American people, it must alike clothe itself in some form which carries with it the rhythms and colouring of a new imagination—an imagination which cries with Carl Sandburg,

> I speak of new cities and new people,
> I tell you the past is a bucket of ashes.

John Galsworthy

John Galsworthy

On his first sight of Greenwich Hospital, Carlyle is said to have remarked that above all things it looked the work of a gentleman, and I am inclined to think that that criticism embodies the keenest impression felt after a reading of Galsworthy's novels. It is unlikely that any satisfactory definition of a gentleman will ever be made, but there are certain qualities of mind and heart for which no better name ever seems to present itself. Reserve, sensitiveness, dignity, honour, are such qualities: a nature which would never descend to an obvious personal attack in a work of fiction, such as that of which one of our leading modern novelists is undeniably guilty: a nature again which would never be moved to any emotion of delight, however naïvely boyish, at the spectacle of the splendours and luxuries of a giant hotel. . . . Galsworthy's novels are the work of such a man. It is work which it is extraordinarily difficult to criticize and to value justly. Sometimes it seems as if it possesses everything except the one thing needful—the gift which should transmute his sentiment into passion and his fineness of drawing into real artistic vigour. He has so much. His thought is sound and sincere; his sensibility delicate; his sympathy profound: his workmanship and sense of form exquisite; and yet, in spite of it all, there is a sense of something lacking in his work as a whole, a feeling not exactly of narrowness, but of smallness and spareness of effect, something a little meagre, a lack of robustness, of vitality, which is disconcerting. Disconcerting because the charm of Galsworthy's quietness and modesty and deep sincerity is such that one is anxious to admire his work in a spirit of the most whole-hearted appreciation. And somehow one cannot. The restraint, which is at once his strength and yet his greatest weakness, is felt everywhere in his art. An extreme example of what I mean is that he himself states that he regards as the greatest moment in his creation that moment in the last act of *Strife* when old John Anthony and David Roberts bow to each other in mutual defeat. A moment without words. But for the greatest achievement of a man of letters to be a moment of silence, has something contradictory and perverse about it.

Galsworthy, like all the great writers of the present day except Conrad, is a satirist, or more truly an ironist towards his own epoch. Like Bernard Shaw, Wells, and Bennett, he looks round on what man has made of man and sees that it is very bad. In his plays, Galsworthy's scope for satire is very wide and his sense of irony plays on almost every class in the community of to-day; in his novels, however, his butt is a much smaller one. Like his fellow artists he is still criticizing the various forms of the English mind, the national prejudices, beliefs, and traditions which form the fundamental ideas of its Victorian civilization; but he traces the colouring of the entire age to a few representative groups—small in actual numbers, but overwhelming in the power they wield: the governing aristocracy, incarnated in *The Patrician,* the landed gentry in *The Country House,* the moneyed professional classes in *The Forsyte Saga,* and (much less important) the moneyed intellectuals in *Fraternity.* It is the ideas engendered by those strata of society which Galsworthy sees as having made the England of the passing generation. In *The Country House* we have an exposition of the working of the Pendyce creed:

"I believe in my father, and his father, and his father's father, the makers and keepers of my estate, and I believe in myself and my son and my son's son. And I believe that we have made the country, and shall keep the country what it is. And I believe in the Public Schools, and especially the Public School that I was at. And I believe in my social equals and the country house, and in things as they are, for ever and ever. Amen."

In Viscount Harbinger in *The Patrician* we see a typical man living by the Public School habit,

that peculiar, extraordinarily English habit, so powerful and beguiling that it becomes a second nature stronger than the first—of relating everything in the Universe to the standards and prejudices of a single class. Since practically all his intimate associates were immersed in it, he was naturally not in the least conscious of this habit, indeed there was nothing

he deprecated so much in politics as the narrow and prejudiced outlook, such as he had observed in the Nonconform-
ist or labour politician. . . .

Lord Valleys, again, is what Pepys would call "vexed
to the blood" by the extraordinary behaviour of his
son, Lord Miltoun.

. . . his way too of acting on his principles! Why! He
even admitted that he acted on his principles! This thought
always struck a very discordant note in Lord Valleys' breast.
It was almost indecent; worse—ridiculous! The fact was,
the dear fellow had unfortunately a deeper habit of thought
than was wanted in politics—dangerous—very!

The ideal patrician behaviour being to act like Lady
Casterley, to realize that this world is a place of facts,
and to reject instinctively any of those foolish practices
of introspection, contemplation, and understanding so
deleterious to authority. Even Barbara's faith is much
the same—to stand no nonsense in herself or others—
"not to slop over anywhere." They are all equally
afraid of powerful thinking and of powerful feeling: sucked dry by a system. But far the most powerful
system of all is the Forsyte system, which lies em-
balmed in Galsworthy's most famous book, *The Forsyte Saga*. What Arnold Bennett did for lower middle-
class society in *The Old Wives' Tale*, Galsworthy does
for upper middle-class society in *The Forsyte Saga*.
One is the epic of the Five Towns: the other of the
London bourgeoisie.

André Chevrillon says the book may almost be classified as zoology, for we have in it an entire branch of the human race presenting both its specific and its individual features. We follow the Forsyte mind through its most general and its most particular workings: we see all the Forsyte doings, morning, noon, and night; we follow their concepts of life and death, of happiness, of honour, of conduct, of religion, of love, of art. We see the family "in full plumage" at At Homes, dinners, weddings, and funerals: we see them gossiping in their homes about each other's business; dreaming of the past and planning for the future; doing good and ill; acting and suffering according to their generic creed and their individual characters. It is a class "pickled in a self-preserving egotism," slaves to a sense of property which includes their money, their houses, their reputations, their wives, their children, and their individual health and happiness. They never lose hold of this sense, becoming in extreme old age like Aunt Ann, bedrid and senile, but still hugging her hoard of Forsyte family possessions: "all their little secrets, illnesses, engagements, and marriages, how they are getting on, whether they were making money: all this was her property, her life." They are instinctively unable to give themselves, body and soul, to anything outside themselves: instinctively unable to appreciate anything which cannot be assessed in terms of money. Art, for instance, means the selling value of works of art.

"Of course Soames is a connoisseur," said Aunt Julie. "He has wonderful taste. He can always tell beforehand what's going to be successful."

Land means the selling value of a piece of land. When June asks James Forsyte why he doesn't go into the country,

"Why," began James in a flutter, "what good d'you suppose I could do, buying land, building houses? I couldn't get four per cent for my money."

"What does that matter? You'd get fresh air."

"Fresh air! What should I do with fresh air?"

They have an instinctive belief in precedent, going along like James, "with his nose, like the nose of a sheep, fastened to the pasture on which he browsed": they never speculate impersonally and discuss ideas, having minds, like Swithin's, "where very little took place from morning till night"; and they have an instinctive dread of anything foreign to themselves—the attitude we see them in at the At Home which opens *The Man of Property*, where they are "like a herd of animals, sniffing danger in the air, but as yet not quite sure what it is that threatens." It is the arrival of that dangerous creature, an artist, in their midst, as June's lover, which is affecting them thus, and their feeling towards the whole thing is summed up in Aunt Hester's remark about Bosinney's coming to pay a formal call in a soft grey hat which she has mistaken for a cat and tried to "shoo" off a chair. "So extraordi-

nary, my dear, so odd." They all live to be very, very
old, because "never to see yourself as others see you
is a wonderful preservative," and their energy, tenacity,
invincible vitality, and pride of place and property and
name has something magnificent in its solidity. They
are the pillars of the state, the cornerstones of conven-
tionality, and everything that is admirable, says young
Jolyon, half laughing and half serious, and as even
Bosinney himself says, "you can't have self-respect
without regularity, either in life or in architecture."
The weakness of the Forsytes is, of course, that that
regularity has become a mere formal one with most of
them, it does not rest on any vital spirit of unity. And
as generation succeeds generation, the family splits,
just as, at Aunt Ann's funeral, the wind blew up the
hill "like some slow disintegrating force" and the
mourners straggled away in groups. This resistless
force is the new character of the younger generation.
It has lost the convictions and assurances of its parents
and grandparents, it has become more self-conscious
and self-critical, more imaginative, more alert, more in-
trospective—losing the solid family tenacity of its for-
bears—like them only in that it still cherishes the
traditional possessive instinct, hugs its prejudices and
egotisms and worldly goods, and likes to suck the fruits
of life and throw away the rinds.

All Galsworthy's books centre in a conflict—in a situation where the instinct for conformity finds itself at
odds with some powerful disintegrating force. It is

this centralization of interest which makes him so beloved of French critics. He has none of that desultory
realism so frequent in English novelists, which makes
them the despair of French readers. Each story is developed from an idea, and springs from a definite crisis
of the human spirit. His aim, he says, is to present
truth, as he sees it, so that it shall produce in his read·
ers "a sort of mental and moral ferment, whereby
vision may be enlarged and understanding promoted."
And he seems to see the truth of life as a series of effects planned by some great artist in irony. He sees
men "like flies, caught among the impalpable and
smoky threads of cobwebs," struggling in those webs
of their own natures and of their environment, "giving
here a start, there a pitiful small jerking, long sustained and then falling into stillness. Enmeshed they
were born, enmeshed they die, fighting according to
their strength to the end." This brooding, melancholy
sense of irony is the most obvious characteristic of
Galsworthy's writing: this view of human beings en-
snared by the implacable cruelty of life, and unaware
of their own helplessness in its trap. He sees them
like Soames, imagining that reason and prudence can
prevent anything. "How could he fall, when his soul
abhorred the circumstances which render a fall possible? A man cannot fall off the floor." Relentlessly,
Galsworthy illustrates first the social and moral systems which man has evolved through the ages to safe-
guard his well-being against possible attack, and then

the weakness of such systems in the face of individual emotional experience. Particularly the experience of love, for that is the situation in all the best known of his novels. On the one hand there is man's fierce desire to regulate the lives of other people by tradition, convention, and prejudice—on the other side the lawlessness of passion. *The Forsyte Saga*, says its author, does not set out to recreate a period. That is its setting, but its central idea is eternal—it is "the disturbance that Beauty effects in the lives of men. . . . The figure of Irene . . . is a concretion of disturbing Beauty impinging on a possessive world."

It is an illustration of Galsworthy's sentimentality that he prefers to call sexual love Beauty, but certainly that is the force which in the person of Irene is fighting Forsytism throughout the book, and appears over and over again in the novels; the force which is vanquished by fate in *The Man of Property;* by compassion at the end of *The Dark Flower;* by tradition in *The Patrician;* by its own decay in *The Country House;* by overcivilization in *Fraternity;* by the past in *To Let.* There is a deep pathos in the pictures of these poor souls who are sensitive enough to feel the chains of their traditions, but too weak to escape from them, Lord Miltoun and Lady Barbara, Hilary Dallison, Olive Cramier, and so on. A great sense of melancholy impotence and waste, but there is something innately unsatisfactory in Galsworthy's treatment of this problem. "Love is a wild plant, springing from wild seed, blown along the road by a wild wind. . . . Where this wild plant springs men and women are but moths around the pale flamelike blossom." But as a matter of fact it isn't its wildness we think of a bit in Galsworthy. It is impossible to think of a less suitable word to describe its quality. Pity, not terror, is what he brings to his tragic situations, and indeed his pity for any suffering is the most obvious characteristic of his personality, after his all-pervading irony. He sees human beings divided from each other by unnecessary selfishness and ignorance and folly and cruelty, and he is filled with an over-flowing compassion for anything that is weak or hurt. As one critic remarks caustically, but candidly, "the very sight of a butterfly makes him think of wheels!" Some one has said that an artist does not represent life, but discerns a certain quality in it, which colours his view of it and expresses his own personality. If that is so, Galsworthy discerns the quality of pathos, which makes it impossible for him to mock whole-heartedly at any human creature. I cannot imagine Galsworthy scourging the money changers of the Temple. He sees that Soames Forsyte and Mr. Pendyce, Lord Valleys and Bianca Dallison are all victims themselves rather than sinners, and though it is always obvious which side he himself favours, he never shows, for example, any of Wells's direct impatience and anger against human stupidity. Nor again, does he supply any exact doctrine to replace our present muddle, though his faith is implicit in all he writes and he has, in one of his last prefaces, gone a little beyond his usual impenetrable reserve in the expression of his beliefs. He sees, he says, no cause for gloom in the mere fact of life's mystery.

> Life for those who still have vital instinct in them is good enough in itself even if it lead to nothing, and we humans have only ourselves to blame if we, alone among animals, so live that we lose the love of life for itself. As for the parts we play, courage and kindness seem to me the only virtues. . . .

The last sentence is elaborated somewhat by Courtier, in *The Patrician*, answering Lord Miltoun's exposition of the necessity of authority, by declaring that God is within the world, not outside it, and that the world is ruled not by power, but by love. "Society is held together by the natural decency in man, by fellow-feeling. The democratic principle, which you despise, at root means nothing at all but that." Mr. Stone, again, illustrates the infinite pathos of mere individual moral greatness, unrelated to practical fellowship. Fraternity is not a thing to write of; it is a thing to live, and there is a little descriptive passage in that book which conveys, as Galsworthy's descriptive passages so often do, the emotional significance of the whole story.

> Outside, in the dark gardens, the moon hung full and almost golden. Its honey-pale light filtered down on every little shape and tree and leaf and sleeping flower. That

soft, vibrating radiance seemed to have woven all into one mysterious whole, stilling disharmony, so that each little separate shape had no meaning to itself.

If we turn from an examination of Galsworthy's ideas in general, to an examination of his creative faculty in scene and character, in the novels themselves, we find ourselves again face to face with that vague dissatisfaction of which I have already spoken. There is a sensation of never getting to grips with the emotion all through the stories. One longs for him to let himself go, and plunge his characters in speech and action into the torrent of intensity which we feel instinctively *should* engulf them. He is a brilliant artist in situation. He states a problem, examines it from conflicting points of view, illustrates the way it influences different lives and affects different philosophies —but there it stays. It is, in a sense, a heavy handicap to him, that he sets himself to picture the minds and spirits of a class of people whose traditional code is the suppression of any signs of emotion, but the effect is sometimes almost that of a deliberate shirking, a fastidious shrinking from direct emotional clashes. The result is that the stories illustrate in general the presence of certain ideas and certain forces in life, rather than the essential emotions of certain individuals. The characters never take the story into their own hands. They are too typical to be quite individual. So many of the leading parts are played by figures that stand for an idea as well as for a human being, and it detracts from their actuality. To me Lord Miltoun, Mark Lennan, George Pendyce, Courtier, Bosinney, and young Jon Forsyte are vague figures. Old Jolyon is Galsworthy's great living creation; he has been very successful, too, with Michael Mont, and the whole group in *Fraternity* have a certain crisp reality about them; while he seldom fails to portray the characters he dislikes—Soames, for instance, or old Mr. Pendyce—with a very firm outline.

Otherwise it is in small flashes that he excels. The picture of the solemn old peacock, Swithin Forsyte, driving Irene down to Robin Hill; old James Forsyte, aged ninety, declaring "we never had any trouble with *our* wives"—or an illuminating morsel of dialogue: " 'Uncle Soames never misses a train,' said Val. 'Why should I?' said Soames."

The typical Galsworthy women all have the same characteristics: creamy-skinned, dark-eyed, slim-fingered creatures, with a magnetic softness and glamorous mystery haunting them, and a power of passive gentle endurance. I suppose some people find them convincing, and know such women. Women who, in spite of their *extreme* delicacy of sensibility, always seem to have married without love: who live in flower-embowered houses or flats: dress in full evening dress with a bunch of fresh violets in the *corsage* when they are quite alone, and spend perfumed passionate existences playing the piano, till the lover appears, bringing some fate which can never possibly be settled by a straightforward divorce, and plunging them both forthwith into death or despair or disappearance. This is the typical Galsworthy woman and her fate, but there are others. Margery Pendyce is a really charming creation, with her tender dignity and invincible gentleness, and the little model in *Fraternity* with what one critic calls her "meek vulgarity" of mind is a very skilful little sketch. Galsworthy's cleverest portrait, however, is, I think, that of June Forsyte—perhaps because he obviously does not really like her! She really lives; from the first time we see her—engaged to Bosinney—all hair and spirit, with her Viking-coloured eyes, so downright, so courageous, so determined to have her own way, with "something in her which suggested a thin Skye terrier just before its dinner." And thence all through her life, surrounded by the "lame ducks" she spends her time trying to help, innately unlovable, dressed in a ridiculous djibbah, managing and "bossy," but always holding her head high and keeping a flag flying in her heart. We see her very well at Fleur's wedding.

"Tell me, didn't Irene spoil your life too?"

June looked up. "Nobody can spoil a life, my dear. That's nonsense. Things happen, but we bob up. . . . Don't sit down under it. We can't control life, but we can fight it—I've had to. I've held on . . . and I've cried—and look at me!"

But Galsworthy's success with character is only occasional and his greatest strength in his representation of life is his creation of the *atmosphere* of a scene or a mood. Perhaps the amount of suggestion which he manages to infuse into description goes far to make up for his weakness in the direct dramatic creation of character. His masterpiece is the picture of old Jolyon Forsyte in *The Indian Summer of a Forsyte,* and that immortal spirit of the mysterious, the unknown, incarnate in a beautiful woman, which makes life seem like a draught of wine to him at eighty-five, which makes loveliness defeat reason in his spirit, and gives the flowers and sunlight and all life a livelier value to him as the spirit of anticipation stirs in his old heart again. The sweetness of the scene where he looks at little Holly, sleeping, and the exquisite grace of his passing as he waits happily for Irene to come to him through the garden, are unforgettable. Indeed, when one begins to think of individual moments in the Galsworthy novels, the mind is thronged with vivid pictures: Courtier's sensations as he sits in the Park and sees Barbara and Harbinger pass arm-in-arm; Mrs. Pendyce's visit to her son's room in Chelsea; the mute, distressful meeting of Bianca and Hilary Dallison in her room; the dinner party when June first realizes that Bosinney and Irene are in love; the extraordinarily moving episode of Soames Forsyte trying to warm his dying father's feet: old Jolyon standing beside the dead body of Bosinney in the mortuary or the return

of Irene to Soames's house when she has heard of
Bosinney's death. Soames comes in and sees her sitting in her usual corner of the sofa.

He shut the door softly, and went towards her. She did not
move, and did not seem to see him.

"So you've come back?" he said. "Why are you sitting
here in the dark?"

Then he caught sight of her face, . . . and her eyes, that
looked enormous, like the great, wide, startled brown eyes
of an owl.

Huddled in her grey fur against the sofa cushions, she had
a strange resemblance to a captive owl, bunched in its soft
feathers against the wires of a cage. The supple erectness
of her figure was gone, as though . . . there were no longer
any reason for being beautiful, and supple, and erect. . . .

Suddenly she tried to rise, but he prevented her; it was
then that he understood.

She had come back like an animal wounded to death, not
knowing where to turn, not knowing what she was doing. . . .

He knew then for certain that Bosinney had been her
lover; knew that she had seen the report of his death—perhaps, like himself, had bought a paper at the draughty
corner of a street, and read it.

. . . he longed to cry: "Take your hated body, that I love,
out of my house! Take away that pitiful white face, so
cruel and soft . . . Get out of my sight; never let me see
you again!"

And, at those unspoken words, he seemed to see her rise
and move away, like a woman in a terrible dream . . . —
rise and go out into the dark and cold, without a thought of
him, without so much as the knowledge of his presence.

Then he cried, contradicting what he had not yet spoken,
"No; stay there!" And turning away from her, he sat down

in his accustomed chair on the other side of the hearth. They sat in silence.

And Soames thought: "Why is all this? Why should I suffer so? What have I done? It is not my fault."

Again he looked at her, huddled like a bird that is shot and dying . . .

So they sat, by the firelight, in the silence, one on each side of the hearth.

There is, indeed, no modern writer who can suggest the atmosphere of passion through description that Galsworthy can. That terrible picture of Lord Miltoun watching Mrs. Noel from the darkness of her garden:

He suddenly found his hand up at his mouth, as though there were blood there to be staunched that had escaped from his heart.

Still holding that hand before his mouth, and smothering the sound of his feet in the long grass, he crept away.

Or poor Soames looking at Irene's photograph in his old age: "the owl hooted, the red climbing roses seemed to deepen in colour, there came a scent of lime blossom"—and the memory of his old passion breaks over him . . . or the haunting sadness of the glimpses we get of Irene and Bosinney and their star-crossed love.

All one, too, with this genius for suggesting the spirit of passion, is his use of background. Round all his lovers hovers a spirit distilled from all that is beautiful in external nature. We feel it in the ecstasy of Audrey Noel and Eustace Miltoun.

The feel of his arms round her, the strength and passion of that moment, were so terribly sweet, that she died to thought, just looking up at him, with lips parted and eyes darker with the depths of her love than he had ever dreamed that eyes could be. . . . It was very still in the room; the roses and carnations in the lustre bowl, seeming to know that their mistress was caught up into heaven, had let their perfume steal forth and occupy every cranny of the abandoned air; a hovering bee, too, circled round the lovers' heads, scenting, it seemed, the honey in their hearts.

Over so many of the books there is a strange brooding sense of a summer evening—an atmosphere of the passionate perfumed dusk which blots out the figures of the lovers, even as they hide their love from the eyes of the world. We have it most exactly described in *The Dark Flower:*

From the field came the scent of hay and the heavy scent of meadowsweet: the musky odour of the backwater was confused with them into one brooding perfume. How still and warm was the air, yet seemed to vibrate against his cheek as though about to break into flame. . . .

All things waited. The creatures of night were slow to come forth after that long bright summer's day, watching for the shades of the trees to sink deeper and deeper into the now chalk-white water: watching for the chalk-white face of the sky to be masked with velvet. The very black plumed trees themselves seemed to wait in suspense for the grape bloom of night. All things stared, wan in that hour of passing day—all things had eyes, wistful and unblessed.

Those last words, I think, sum up the picture of humanity which Galsworthy's work leaves in the mind:

"wistful and unblessed": all the hopeless, ironic, gloom of his mind: "the heartbreak at the heart of things." He loves Beauty, but his heart is dominated by the sadness underlying all beauty; by the heaviness of heart its swift passing brings; by the pathos of its short perfection. Those are the thoughts that Galsworthy leaves: the inexorable sadness of things—that melancholy who—

> Dwells with Beauty—Beauty that must die
> And Joy, whose hand is ever at his lips
> Bidding adieu.

H. G. Wells

H. G. Wells

WHEN Mr. Swinnerton first published *Nocturne*, the book appeared with a preface by H. G. Wells, and in that preface Wells contrasts his own literary methods with those illustrated by Swinnerton's masterpiece. After commenting on "that beauty which comes from exquisite presentation" he goes on to say:

> Personally I have no use at all for life as it is, except as raw material. It bores me to look at things unless there is also the idea of doing something with them. . . . In the books I have written, it is always about life being altered I write, or about people developing schemes for altering life. And I have never once "presented" life. My apparently most objective books are criticisms and incitements to change.

Wells has as great a distrust of Art for Art's Sake as Shaw himself. Art for Society's Sake might be his motto and he is constantly reminding his public of his ideal; telling Henry James, "To you literature is an end, like painting: to me it is a means, like architecture; it has a use"; or declaring that he would rather be called a journalist than an artist; or pointing out that, since a novel leaves impressions, not only of things seen, but of acts judged and made attractive or the reverse, therefore it has an inseparable moral consequence. Like Remington he is determined to get experience for humanity out of his talent, and bury nothing, like Mr. Britling, though it seems at times plain to him that he is a "weak, silly, ill-informed, and hasty-minded writer," he nevertheless has the conviction that the spirit of God is in him, and that it falls to him "to take some part in the establishment of a new order of living upon earth," to use his richness of mind for the definite end of a great purpose—the ideal of a nobler civilization.

He suffers [says Mr. Mencken] from a Messianic delusion, and once a man suffers from a Messianic delusion, his days as a serious artist are ended.

Mr. Wells, however, will at any rate enjoy the company of the Hebrew prophets, Milton, Bunyan, and Bernard Shaw, so perhaps he will survive being called a brummagem prophet by Mr. Mencken.

The critics, especially the American critics, do not seem to like Mr. Wells. Stuart Sherman makes him out to be the dispenser of a kind of worthless, dishonest, moral Tono Bungay; a social poison so obviously unwholesome that he declares that it is only acceptable to "radicals of one and twenty, and middle-aged women with imaginations unappeased by experience." Moreover, he is frankly impatient at Wells's inability to come to any final and definite conclusions. Mr. Sherman is evidently one of those whom Mr. Britling describes as finding him "seriously exasperating," but

really this open-mindedness is one of Wells's most attractive traits, more especially in the face of the number of rigid little dogmatists who think that since the
publication of *The Outline of History* they can afford
to be arrogantly superior towards him. He is always
open to conviction and he cannot resist ideas: there
seems moreover to be a notice addressed to ideas put
up in his mind saying, "Don't Park Here." His love
of altering things extends to his own opinions. I am
sure he would agree with Stevenson that to travel hope-
fully is better than to arrive, and he says himself that
the really hopeless thing about George Ponderevo's
wife was that she "had no faculty for growth or
change." Of course there is no doubt that Wells very
frequently is exasperating. Often, as I think Mr. J. B.
Priestley has said somewhere, one feels his attitude
to Society is that crystallized in the remark, "Go and
see what Baby is doing and tell him not to": often, as
in *The Dream,* he is in that mood when a man goes
out for a walk and slashes the tops of everything with
his cane: often he scolds the social system as if it
were a delinquent schoolchild. But in spite of all that,
how immeasurably the balance is on the other side!

"I suppose what I'm really trying to render is nothing more nor less than life, as one man has found it,"
says George Ponderevo, and in his fifty-odd books that
is what Wells has tried to do. It is the life of a man
who before he was twenty-seven had lived in a back
shop in Bromley like Remington; had been a child at

Bladesover, like George; had served in a drapery establishment like Kipps and Mr. Polly; had been a student at South Kensington like Mr. Lewisham and a demonstrator like Capes in *Ann Veronica;* and who since then has shown the ceaseless intellectual alertness of a Bernard Shaw, the ceaseless energy of a Benvenuto Cellini, and the ceaseless interest in life of a Samuel Pepys.

"Promise me" [says Lady Mary in *The Passionate Friends*], "promise me, Stephen, here and now, never to be grey and grubby: never to be humpy and snuffy, never to be respectable and modest and dull and a little fat—like everybody."

"Directly a crust forms on things, you are restless to break down to the fire again," says [Margaret of Remington.]

"I want to get as near as I can to the thrill of a dog going into a fight, or the delight of a bird in the air."

All these quotations suggest something of the courageous, gusty, high-spirited, challenging disposition of their writer. His opinions, as Mr. Chesterton says, are never conclusive, but always suggestive: each is a good starting point for thought, if only for the thought which refutes it. . . . Nobody else can make such splendid stuff out of the very refuse of his rejected opinions. He has a perfect lust to take hold of life and create from it, not just to think about it, but to be constantly testing it on experience, experimenting with formulas and making his mind a laboratory for the trial of new beliefs, so that Van Wyck Brooks says that Wells has done for the social organism what Wordsworth did for Nature, that is, discovered a thing previously felt to be inanimate, as matter for art and a basis for religious emotion—a personality. I don't think there is a single side of modern life omitted from his re-creation of the age in his novels—politics, war, the country-house, the business world, the middle-class shopkeeper, science, education, feminism, sex. Everything is in those amazing books. He creates every class in the social system, probes that system, or lack of system, to its heart, and yet presents the whole with a vivid colouring of his own personality.

But Wells, as he says, is not interested particularly in the presentation as such, brilliantly though he does it. While he says truly that he renders life as one man has found it, his real interest is to render it as one man hopes to make it. He regards the epoch and the human beings living in it exactly as he regards the whole history of the world, as raw material only, as things to do something with, as incidents in a vast race drama, whose course can be influenced and altered, by the power of his thought and his word. He and Arnold Bennett in their respective outlooks on their own epoch suggest somewhat the relation of Chaucer and Langland in the fourteenth century. Bennett takes life as he finds it and things as they are. Sane and good-tempered, he sees men and women, fine or base, cloddish or noble. Their natures and motives interest him intensely, but quite tolerantly. He is placid and serene and untormented by moral judgments: aloof and detached. He sees that men are petty and women light, that they are stupid, and narrow, and cruel, but at the same time that they are kind and unselfish, pitiful, and just, and that there is always love and faith, spring and music in the world, and the indomitable toughness of the human spirit. Wells has none of this serenity. He cannot be calm about the world he finds himself face to face with. He is appalled by it, and he cannot keep his temper before the spectacle of its baseness. He must set down the burning facts about the exploitation and oppression of the poor; the ill-adjustments of the forces of capital and labour, the injustice of the social code, the hypocrisy of the political world, the cruelty of the lunacy laws. He must protest passionately that such things *must* be changed and the honour of humanity vindicated; and something in his spirit drives him perpetually to employ his teeming mind on constructive ideas and Utopian philosophies on the theme that there is no Being but Becoming.

We haven't got the right system, but there is a right system possible, none the less. The Spirit of Order, the spirit that has already produced organized Science will in the long run certainly save mankind.

Wells is far too sane an observer to imagine, as some of his critics pretend, that any sociological legislation is going to reform mankind.

I have long since ceased to trouble about the economics of human society. Ours are not economic, but psychological difficulties. . . . Beings are unique: circumstances are unique and therefore we cannot think of regulating our conduct by wholesale dicta."

But like Shaw he insists over and over again that no development is possible unless society will be intellectually honest, and face all knowledge about itself unblinkingly, discussing, analyzing, illuminating conduct through and through. He sees the average man at present, never speaking openly about the really important matters in life. "It is like wearing gloves in summer fields or bathing in a gown." Wells, like social reformers of all ages and nationalities, declares over and over again that the human consciousness has got to be freed from the grooves of tradition, the hypnotic suggestions of authority, the parochial influences of immediate surroundings and the dogmatisms of the popular press. At present "Society cares more for dead rules than for living men," he exclaims angrily, and in the heroes of *Marriage, Tono Bungay,* and *The New Machiavelli* he shows the fine, constructive, serving, disinterested type of man forced out of his true work by the pressure of some special social limitation, moral or economic. At the same time he sees the business world ruled by the principles of grab and greed; the political world by self-interest; the international world by false patriotisms: all just muddling through in a universe full of individuals with no common purpose, no organized collective mind, no proud dreams and proud lusts, no spirit in them. A universe peopled with men like Bert Smallways in *The War in the Air:*

a vulgar little creature, the sort of pert, limited soul that the civilizations of the early twentieth century produced by the million in every country. . . . He thought the whole duty of man was to be smarter than his fellows, get his hands, as he put it, on the dibs, and have a good time,

while those who were less smart are like the pathetically futile Kipps, all of whose tragedy Wells sees under his mask of humour, and expresses in the bitter outburst towards the end of the book, when, after describing the silly little quarrel between Kipps and Ann, he suddenly cries:

You think I'm going to write fat, silly, grinning novels about half-educated, under-trained people, and keep it up all the time, that the whole thing's nothing but funny!

As I think of them lying unhappily there, my vision pierces the night. See what I can see! Above them, brooding over them, I tell you there is a monster, a lumpish monster, . . . like all that is darkening and heavy and obstructive in life. It is the . . . anti-soul, . . . Stupidity. My Kippses live in its shadow. Shalford and his apprenticeship system, the Hastings Academy, the ideas of Coote, the ideas of the old Kippses, all the ideas that have made Kipps what he is, all these are a part of its shadow. But for that monster they might not be groping among false ideas and hurt one another so sorely; but for that, the glowing promise of childhood and youth might have had a happier fruition, thought might have awakened in them to meet the thought of the world, . . . their lives might not have been divorced as now they are divorced, from the apprehension of beauty that we favoured ones are given . . . I laugh at these two people; I have sought to make you laugh. . . .

But I see through the darkness the souls of my Kippses as they are, . . . as things like the bodies of little, ill-nourished, ailing, ignorant children, children who feel pain, who are naughty and muddled and suffer and do not understand why.

The centre of gravity in the whole fabric of Wells's social beliefs, the basis on which all his social thought is built, is his unshakable conviction that man has his future in his own hands, and that the vast majority of youthful mankind is full of undeveloped fineness. He sees, he says, more than half the youth of the world like George Ponderevo when he first came to London:

Rather dangerously open-minded and open-eyed but with something fine in me, seeking fine responses. I did not want simply to live happily and well. I wanted to serve and do and make—with some nobility.

This being so, man can mould civilization into something more worthy of his youthful ideals: he can alter anything if he have motive enough and faith enough: "there is no circumstance in the world which determined action cannot alter." It is this assurance which informs all his romances, the sense of the infinite plasticity of things: the fact that the universe is not fixed and static, but is malleable by man; that anything may happen if humanity wills it. In *The History of Mr.*

Polly we have a complete parable of Wells's view of Man and society. We are introduced to poor Mr. Polly, sitting on a gate, suffering from acute indigestion, finding the universe nothing but a "beastly silly 'ole." "Untrained, unwarned, confused, distressed, angry, seeing nothing except that he was, as it were, netted in greyness and discomfort, with life dancing all around him," and a conviction in that dim little mind of his that somewhere there was interest and happiness and beauty and delight in the world. And Mr. Polly makes a marvellous discovery. He had always been "the skeptaceous sort" and suspected that it is only the results of actions which make them good or bad, and we certainly agree that his deliberate burning of his house and shop was not evil but good. Especially as he followed it up by absconding and making the great discovery, *If the world does not please you, you can change it altogether*. He does change it, finding happiness at the Potwell Inn and being filled with amazement to think he had endured his monotony of misery and failure so long. But he has to win his final peace. Apollyon "straddles quite across the way" in the person of Uncle Jim, and, face to face with that knowledge, Mr. Polly knew—"he knew now as much as a man can know of life. He knew he had to fight or perish. . . ."

The reality of the case arched over him like the vault of the sky, as plain as the sweet blue heavens above, and the wide spread of hill and valley about him. Man comes into life to seek and find his sufficient beauty, to serve it, to win and increase it, to fight for it, to face anything and dare anything for it, counting death as nothing so long as the dying eyes still turn to it. And fear, and dulness and indolence and appetite . . . are against him, to delay him, to hold him off, to hamper and beguile and kill him in that quest.

Wells's hope for the future is that there will be enough faithful fighters finally to defeat these monsters so rampant in the world of men. He sees the present age as an age of crumbling and confusion, of a bubbling up and medley of futile institutions and individuals—but through it all he sees *something*, just as George Ponderevo saw something, in that voyage of his down the Thames, at the end of *Tono Bungay*. It is something that drives, persistently, undeviatingly, through the confusion of the present world. George Ponderevo saw it incarnated in his destroyer, stark and swift, the spirit of Science and Truth—patient, disinterested. But he recognized it everywhere: saw how some men served it in literature, some in art, some in sociology, and how it is the heart of life, the one enduring thing, though nations and epochs and civilizations all pass and pass. . . . The only hope for the world therefore is that this spirit should never die, but should increase and multiply upon the earth, and Wells's finest and most impassioned plea for its continuance is in *The Undying Fire*—a book not very much known, but the clearest and most moving statement of his faith he has ever written. There, in the conversations of the modern types who re-enact the story of Job, he smashes the lifeless codes of his opponents and affirms his own unconquerable belief. Sir Eliphaz holds the view that some vague immortality explains everything in the universe—that the part to play is that of the trusting child who leaves everything to a fatherly God in heaven. Dr. Barrack argues that the Process, i.e., Evolution, is beyond all human knowledge and control:

"It has scrawled our race across the black emptiness of space, and it may wipe us out again. . . . We can but follow our lights and instincts."

Both believe in taking the world as they find it, in making the best of it all, in bowing to the thing that *is*. But Mr. Huss won't:

"I don't submit. I rebel—not in my own strength nor by my own impulse. I rebel by the spirit of God in me. I rebel not merely to make weak gestures of defiance against the black disorder and cruelties of space and time, but for mastery. . . . I am the servant of a rebellious and adventurous God who may yet bring order into this cruel and frightful chaos."

This struggle of his has a hope of victory, but no assurance. Dr. Barrack's Process has a will which he thinks will take man *some*where, but Mr. Huss holds that there is no will, except in and through ourselves. He sees men continuing to live, to follow their own lights, to take the world as they find it, because they do not realize that they are but parts in one great adventure in space and time. He sees a vast amount of human energy and vitality being devoted to things which lead straight to a repetition of a world war. And sees moreover that there is no organized impulse to evil behind such efforts, that the men who are doing such work are probably kindly, good men, but each is taking the world as he finds it. And he illustrates with the powerful story of the young German on the submarine—and sees all mankind as part of the same story. The eternal story of youth and hope and possibility misled, wasted, and lost.

Mr. Huss is a schoolmaster, and Wells dedicates the book "To All the Teachers in All the World," seeing human history as a race between education and catastrophe: the generations rushing to waste, unless the teachers of the world can create an aristocracy of purpose and of understanding, can instil an idea of service into the collective mind of the future, can make it realize that Man is the Thought of the world. Civilization, he says, is a matter of the prevailing ideas, and the problem is, how to make the right ideals prevail. This depends on our teachers, since the whole of mankind is made up of individual Joans and Peters and the sum of civilization is the sum of what we have made of all our Joans and Peters. At present in the world, folly and hate can bawl sanity out of hearing; we turn out "mental cripples" by the million, and in-

stead of spending the years of school life in an attempt
to elucidate the laws of nature and its forces and of
the world of men and their ways, to lift the mind out
of blind alleys, we spend the time "boiling fossils for
soup," as Wells sums up the average classical cur-
riculum.

Every time a teacher turns out a muddle-headed child,
the world has to bear the burden of an incompetent citizen
for fifty or sixty years.

Give me the schools of the world and I would make a
millennium in half a century.

In the Utopia of *Men Like Gods* there is no Government. "Our Education is our Government," say the
godlike inhabitants.

It must be clear, from the time that it has taken to
give even a most imperfect outline of Wells's social
idealism, that his concern in his novels is very much
more with the problems of the species than of the individual. It is Man in conflict with Society that concerns him very much more than man in conflict with
his fellow human beings or with his own heart. "He
presents life as a tangle and not as a riddle," says one
critic; he emphasizes its muddle, not its mystery, and
there is always the haunting feeling that Wells believes
that if only he could get to work and put the universe
in order (with all the gusto with which he describes
keeping a shop in order, in *Kipps*), all the personal

problems of human relationships would automatically adjust themselves. And although, in theory, Wells allows individuals to work out their own idealisms, in practice they are never shown as having any different ones from his own. One has an uncomfortable suspicion that he does not think any one without a taste for biology can have real honesty of outlook, and in *The Dream,* the inhabitants of Utopia don't seem to do anything except work at scientific problems or get up very early in the mornings to climb the Alps. Neither of which occupations appears at all Utopian to some of us!

Wells indeed has, I think, the type of mind which is more full of democratic theory than of what one might call democratic instinct or emotion. We never feel that he has the radiant, simple love of his fellow human beings which Dickens, for example, possessed in such abundant measure. Just as he is not interested in Life for its own sake, but only as raw material for the principle of Change to work upon, so he is not interested in human beings for their own sakes, but primarily as raw material which can be altered into something useful and intelligent. His creative range in character is neither wide nor rich. Most of his fine books are after the pattern of the *Pilgrim's Progress* (only he prefers to call it *The Research Magnificent*), but the only really vivid character is Christian, who is Wells himself. He is not successful in portraying women. Susan Ponderevo is very real and lovable, but otherwise one always feels that his portraits of women typify the problem of Sex and Society, and are not individuals of flesh and blood. Since he was one of the first novelists to be outspoken on the subject of the relations of the sexes, he has earned a reputation among the bourgeoisie for "immorality." Arnold Bennett tells a story of how he once heard a woman say:

"Wells, no, I draw the line at Wells! He stirs up the dregs. I don't mind froth, but dregs I *will not have.*" And silence reigned, as we stared at the reputation of Wells lying dead on the carpet.

Wells is very sincere and straightforward in his treatment of sexual questions. He is never vulgar, like W. L. George, sinking to bedroom scenes and descriptions of lingerie, and he is never obsessed by abnormalities like D. H. Lawrence. Indeed, it isn't the quality but the quantity of what Mr. Mencken calls his "intellectualized adulteries" that one tires of, just as one tires of the samenesses in his heroes and heroines, and just as one tires of his insistance on blaming Society for *everything*. When he declares of the hero of a recent novel, *The Dream*, "I will not apologize for Henry Mortimer Smith: he was what Society had made him," we feel inclined to retort, impolitely, "Rot!" After all, Mr. Wells started life in much the same society and he is Mr. Wells. Indeed, I fear there is some truth in Mr. Mencken's declaration that Wells the creative artist is dead, for though he cannot be really dull, his books tend increasingly to be full of what Kipps or Mr. Polly would call "argy bargy" about the short-comings of society in general and less and less about the doings of real human beings. His great artistic triumphs belong to the earlier books: scenes like those of the funeral of Mr. Polly's father or Kipps in the London hotel; the suburban garden party at Becken-ham in *Tono Bungay;* or the flight in the airplane. Descriptions like that of the tea in the housekeeper's room at Bladesover; the fight in the window at the Emporium when Parsons tries to put the Spirit of Joy into window-dressing; Sunday at the Frapps'. The joyous humour which described Mr. Edward Ponder-evo's preparations for an advertising campaign:

He became in those days the terror of eminent historians. "Don't want your Drum and Trumpet history. No fear! Not my affair: Nobody's affair now. . . . What I want to know is: In the Middle Ages, did they do Anything for Housemaid's Knee? What did they put in their Hot Baths after Jousting? Was the Black Prince Enamelled or Painted or what? I think myself blackleaded very likely—but *did* they use blackleading so early?" . . .

Characters like Kipps and Mr. Polly, Mr. and Mrs. Edward Ponderevo, the earnest Mr. Coote and the optimistic Mr. Chitterlow—Wells has not written in that vein for more than ten years. More and more we have long descriptions of distressing actualities with the anger of the narrator finally exploding into three dots . . . at the end of each paragraph. Less and less do we have that genius for summing up a person or a thing in a phrase: the artist in "conscientiously untidy tweeds" or the description of Mr. Polly's indigestion; or the remark that he was "in the technical sense of the word, clean shaved"; the school "where the study of bookkeeping and French were pursued (but never effectively overtaken)," or the upbringing where Man was represented as "waiting about for the Judgment day with Satan as busy as a pickpocket in a crowd."

Of late years his sense of the futility of men and things, of their stupidities and meannesses and cruelties and waste of precious material, simply swamps his sense of their absurdity and quaintness and pathetic little generosities. If he were to rewrite *Kipps* now, the one passage of personal comment I have already quoted would be expanded into three hundred pages and the actual dramatic representation of the life of Kipps cut down to a quarter of its present length. I suppose that it is probably the mere passage of years that has affected his imagination. At his back he hears Time's winged chariot drawing near, and he hurries to din against the vast deafness of society all the thoughts which fill his busy mind. For though intellectually he appreciates the vast leisureliness of Time in working out the changes imposed by Man, humanly he hates to die with no obvious differences in all that he lived to alter. But Wells is a living example of the great truth that it isn't what a man thinks or says or does that really matters: it is what he *is*. In his literary work he is an intellectual before he is an artist: instinctively he tries to grasp and interpret life through ideas rather than through experience, and his ideas are far dearer to him than experience as such. But though his books are full of fine artistry and fine thinking, and at his best, he will undoubtedly live as one of the outstanding men of letters of this age, it is not his range of ideas, not his creation of perhaps the most comprehensive picture we have of our own epoch, which make his greatness. It is his spirit. Arnold Bennett declared that what was needed more than anything else in intellectually dishonest and hypocritical England was some one who would tell the truth—and chance it! It might have been told, he says, cynically, or meanly, or tediously, and it would still have been valuable—but what Wells has done is to tell the truth with "a warmth of generosity towards mankind and an inspiring faith in mankind and a priceless and total sincerity." It is not possible to read Wells without a glow of invigoration and hope in the potentialities of humanity: he has such a splendid ferment of eager good will towards his fellows and such an inspiriting rebel fortitude.

"I love the way you carry your tail," says Peter to Joan, and it is difficult for the young and the thoughtful not to feel something of the same thing toward Wells. He is gallant and human.

"I have failed myself a thousand times, but no failure lasts if your faith lasts."

"Only have courage. On the courage in your heart all things depend."

Such energetic and encouraging aphorisms come springing to the mind when one thinks of Wells, and whether a reader agrees or disagrees with the details of his many conversions to his many beliefs, his central faith in man's service to man must always be the basis for all human hope for the world, and Wells may justly say with Confucius:

"Every truth has four corners. As a teacher I give you one corner, and it is for you to find the other three."

Arnold Bennett

Arnold Bennett

The novelist is he who, having seen life, and being so excited by it that he absolutely must transmit his vision to others, chooses narrative fiction as the liveliest vehicle for the relief of his feelings.

—ARNOLD BENNETT.

THERE is certainly no doubt whatever about Arnold Bennett having seen life and having been excited by it. Almost all his books might be entitled "Things That Have Interested Me." He has been interested in an incredible number of things about an incredible number of different sorts of people, and he has always described them with an unflagging zest and energy, whether it is the accidents in building the Underground Railway from Clerkenwell to Euston in 1862, or the medieval miracles of the Virgin Mary, or the details of a guillotine execution, or the symptoms of obscure diseases, or how the pottery furnaces were lighted a hundred years ago, or the running of a boarding-house, or a newspaper, or a financier's office, or a drapery shop, or a printing press, or a City of Pleasure. These things however are externals, and any good journalist could make a description of them readable. The novelist must do more than that. His greatness depends not on his excited observation of life, not on the mere scope of his perceptions, but on their quality: on the distinction of vision, the fineness of mind, he brings to his task. Consciously he does nothing but select and arrange his material, weaving a pattern from the warp of his insight and the woof of his beliefs, but unconsciously his individual genius stamps itself upon the whole; the maker's name is always there, unseen, upon the selvage.

This "philosophy of life" in a man's work, his vision and creation of human existence, which in the end, is the test of its worth and its endurance, need not, of course, be contained in his direct analysis of life's problems. Indeed, with Arnold Bennett, if we judged his literary personality by the lay sermons christened by him "Pocket Philosophies," his vision of life, though full of sound common sense and honesty of outlook, is nothing but a restatement of maxims and aphorisms already better expressed by the sayings of Christ, Epictetus, and Marcus Aurelius. There are nine Pocket Philosophies and they may be distinguished—by their titles. Otherwise they are a triumph of saying the same thing, very often, at considerable length, in a variety of different ways. Their message is an excellent one. He tells us to cultivate our human, physical, and mental mechanism to its utmost perfection, and gives sound advice as to the best way of doing it; on the mental plane, how to stir the mind from the sloth of custom and polish it from the tarnish of years of disuse; on the moral plane how the biggest things in life depend on the perfect adjustment of the smallest, how supremely important is kindliness of heart and the avoidance of moral indignation, with many valuable maxims against grumbling and bad temper and worry, becoming the slaves of habit, judging harshly and running away from life. He is the Walter Camp of the mental and moral organs, illustrating a Daily Dozen for the heart and mind, full of healthy common sense, seeing life in proportion, and anxious that the plain man and woman should realize how through cowardice, conceit, hypocrisy, stupidity, intolerance, and self-pity they get so very much less out of his ordinary existence than they might. But again, the "Pocket Philosophies" are journalism. What they say is true, but what literature does and what journalism does not is to give the truths of life *adequate and memorable expression* in artistic form. The "Pocket Philosophies" stand in the same relation to literature as the Daily Dozen to the Russian Ballet.

Probably the main reason for this failure is the difficulty of making the truths of life appear as living truth in so general a fashion—the intensest interest in the study of living, being the struggle, fresh born in every individual soul, between personality and environment, the ceaseless effort of the ego to harmonize itself with its surroundings. Once plunged into the excitement of watching *this* spectacle, once concerned more with the limitations than with the potentialities of human existence, we find the real Arnold Bennett.

"Every street is a mirror, an illustration, an exposition, an explanation, of the human beings who live in it," he says, and there is no one with a keener sense of the immense importance of the correlation of all phenomena in the judgment of any individual and of any event. But though all phenomena excite him, he stands first and foremost as the creator of one very specified set of phenomena, those connected with the industrial and midland district of England known generally as the Potteries, and christened by Arnold Bennett the Five Towns. If any one thinks of Arnold Bennett, he inevitably thinks of the Five Towns. Of course Bennett constantly creates whole stories outside that setting. He can command the world of Mr. Prohack or the Pretty Lady, groups of kindly, witty, wealthy men, and attractive middle-aged women, young dogs about town, and vivacious, independent girls, in settings of smart society in the London or Paris of to-day. But no one thinks of such books as typical Bennett books. His real world is the world of the solid discomfort of St. Luke's Square, and rows and rows of streets like Freehold Villas, where there was "nothing but narrowness. Long narrow strips of garden and narrow houses all flattened together, and uniformity and brickiness and polished brassiness and an eternal laundry." Places where people keep small shops or collect rents or run boarding-houses, and where

there are revolting old men like Darius Clayhanger
and Mr. Batchgrew and Critchlow the chemist, and old
women like Auntie Hamps who wear "mantles," and
bonnets trimmed with jet fruit and crape leaves. These
men and women are served by young girls, shapeless
in sacking aprons, who slop dirty water over kitchen
floors and wring out steaming cloths with coarse, red-
dened hands, and behind the Nottingham lace curtains
in the parlours they all eat tea at six o'clock, with mut-
ton chops and fried fish and eggs and bacon, seated on
slithery horsehair chairs, surrounded by wool mats,
antimacassars and family Bibles, gloating over death-
beds, funerals, and catastrophes, and considering any
enjoyment outside a Sunday School fête as deliberate
sin.

Talk to Auntie Hamps of lawn tennis or a musical evening, and she would set you down as flighty, and shift the
conversation on to soaps or chapel.

A drab atmosphere, human and physical: all the dirt
and unloveliness of industrialism, with the provincial
stupidity, the inarticulate pessimism, the religious
bigotry and puritan hypocrisy of the English lower
middle class, against the grey, dank, smoky chill of
the English midlands.

Then Bennett takes these drab human beings in their
drab surroundings and shows how the eternal laws of
humanity fulfil themselves in them: how they face, or
fail to face, the eternal problems and the eternal ex-

periences, and how, from the highest to the lowest, ir-
respective of class or calling, life invariably tricks the
individual, filling him or her with ever blossoming
hopes and expectations, smiting him in the end with
the common lot of apparent futility. It is the consciousness of this truth which gives Sophia that pure
and primitive emotion, uncoloured by any moral or
religious quality, which she feels on seeing the dead
body of the husband she has not met for over thirty
years.

She was not sorry that Gerald had wasted his life . . .
The manner of his life was of no importance. What affected
her was that he had once been young, and that he had grown
old and was now dead. That was all. Youth and vigour
had come to that. Youth and vigour always came to that.
Everything came to that. . . . Reflected in the mirror of a
wardrobe near the bed, she glimpsed a tall, forlorn woman
who had once been young and now was old. . . . "Yet a
little while," she thought, "and I shall be lying on a bed
like that. And what shall I have lived for? What is the
meaning of it?"

A little later, Constance, looking at Sophia's body,
analyzes the same frame of mind, and finds the sum of
her existence that "she had lived in honesty and kindliness for a fair number of years, and she had tasted
triumphant hours." There are not many who can say
much more, and what Arnold Bennett brings home all
through his work is that life, in essence, is exactly the
same thing to Constance and her like as to any other
beings in the world. Her husband, Samuel Povey, the

little provincial draper, "illustrates to the observant the vein of greatness which runs through every soul without exception. He embraced a cause, lost it, and died of it," even if that cause was nothing but an unsuccessful effort to save his cousin from the consequences of manslaughter. In the same way we are made to feel that young love is the same thing to Rachel Fores as it is to Juliet: heroisms like that of Hilda Lessways, on the threshold of new love, discovering that she is going to have a child by the bigamist who has pretended to marry her, and facing her fate in silence; miseries like that of Edwin Clayhanger as he waits in vain for some explanation of her silence—there is nothing "provincial" in them. Nor in the solidity of character, honesty, and kindliness of Sophia and Constance and Elsie, qualities which invest their lives with a central dignity which is not greatly smaller than that of a Volumnia or an Imogen.

The meaning of life to Bennett, in so far as the word "meaning" can be applied to so diffused an impression as he leaves, seems to be simply that, though life never fails to cheat the individual, and though the onlooker cannot fail to be filled with an overwhelming sense of the ironic hopelessness of it all, life is nevertheless worth living, simply because each individual instinctively and tenaciously holds it to be so. There is no need to realize desires, it is enough for average human nature to believe that they may be realized—round the next corner: no life is dull unless the liver of that life feels it to be purposeless—a frame of mind very rare among simple people. Arnold Bennett's genius is original in the double vision which he brings to his creation of human consciousness, in his power to combine the sense of ironic detachment from the lives he presents, with, at the same time, a complete identification with them. On the one hand we are made keenly conscious of how environment has warped and prejudiced these minds, how imperfectly they are exercised and trained, how inadequate and superficial and impoverished they are, how much they miss of the potentialities of existence. This is just the impression which Wells also gives us, but Wells leaves us with that impression and nothing more: we never get away from that one point of view. But Bennett goes further. Having shown us these lives as they appear in the light of a sophisticated, cultivated experience, he proceeds to identify himself with his creations, to show how these lives appear to themselves, and how, viewed from that standpoint, nothing is lost to them, because the whole perspective is entirely altered. He comments in *Riceyman Steps* on Elsie and Mr. Earlforward as—

two human beings, both commonplace and both marvellous, bound together and yet incurious each of the other and incurious of the mysteries in which they and all their fellows lived! Mr. Earlforward never asked the meaning of life, for he had a lifelong ruling passion. Elsie never asked the meaning of life, for she was dominated and obsessed by a tremendous instinct to serve. . . .

And then we become identified with each in turn and realize how *complete* a thing life is to each. We get inside the skin of Edwin Clayhanger and understand how setting out on matrimony is as great an adventure for him as setting out to kill the dragon was for St. George. We get inside the skin of Hilda Lessways and know that when she (the only girl in the Five Towns who knew shorthand) ministers to Mr. George Cannon, she feels as indispensable as any priestess ministering to the Sacred Fire. The fact that her activities are, in reality, extremely unimportant, does not make *her* sense of glorification one whit the less. We experience again, with Constance, exactly how vital it seems to decide whether she should meet Sophia in her best or her second-best dress, and how, when she hears the new servant isn't coming, she feels that "actually and truly this was the deepest depths of calamity."

Arnold Bennett's sensitive curiosity of mind delights to probe all the myriad secrets of impulse and motive, all the myriad effects of emotion and intensity of life which lurk under the most forbidding externals, the most apparently impenetrable disguises, and his especial genius as an artist is seen by the skill with which he communicates his own excitement to the reader. It is only necessary to analyze the material of some of his most successful novels to realize the extent of this skill, and to see from what graceless and intractable material he can hew a work of art. In *The Old Wives' Tale*, for instance, we have a story in which the people are all that is dreary and commonplace, in a setting of dingy ugliness and drab respectability, where almost everything that happens is obvious, some of the incidents are positively tedious, there is no suspense in the plot, and the whole is presented with the harshest and most aloof impersonality. Or again, in *Riceyman Steps* we have the history of two sordid misers, living in a squalid court in Clerkenwell, the description of their unpleasant lives and unpleasant illnesses and unpleasant deaths, together with the doings of a clumsy, good-hearted charwoman and her semi-idiot sweetheart. And yet the happy reader feels that he would like the books to go on forever!

There are, no doubt, many people who still agree with the friend who commented on the manuscript of *The Old Wives' Tale* that he thought it honest but dull, and to such it is useless to appeal, for they will never be won to see the passionate romance in Arnold Bennett's realism, the wild poetry in the logic of commonplace character, the mystery curtained by the familiar. They will, perhaps, appreciate his more obvious romance, the jolly extravagance and robust rollicking of *The Card (Denry the Audacious)*; the blithe adroitness and irrepressible good humour of *The Regent (The Old Adam)*; or they may enjoy that quality, which one critic calls provinciality and another boyishness, which makes Arnold Bennett see the splendours of modern London as entrancing as the bazaars of Baghdad, so that the Grand Babylon Hotel appears as wonderful as a Rajah's palace and a Turkish bath as romantic as Constantinople. But this is not the Bennett who, next to Conrad, must rank as the finest artist among English novelists of to-day, the writer whose representation of life, while it lacks the epic breath and virility of the greatest masters, has perhaps more energy, zest, dramatic insight, and variety of scope than any single one of his contemporaries.

It is not possible to claim that Arnold Bennett can suggest the pinnacles and abysses, the heights and depths of human passion. He is not master of these, but of the common pathways of average experience; his emotional power is in his creation of the atmosphere of ordinary happenings to ordinary people, in his re-minting of the commonplace event, in his discovery of the living truth in platitude. Take an effect like his analysis of a mother's feelings on giving up her house to her married daughter—a variant of the eternally comic theme of the mother-in-law, and therefore a subject so difficult to touch without suggesting the taint of the music-hall. This is how he describes Mrs. Baines leaving St. Luke's Square.

Old houses, in the course of their history, see sad sights, and never forget them . . . and the triple house of John Baines saw such on the morning before the afternoon when Mr. and Mrs. Povey returned from their honeymoon—the sight of Mrs. Baines getting into the waggonette for Axe. Mrs. Baines, encumbered with trunks and parcels, leaving the scene of her struggles and her defeat, whither she had once come, slim as a wand, to return stout, and heavy and heavy-hearted, to her childhood, content to live with her grandiose sister until such time as she should be ready for burial. . . . The grimy and impassive old house perhaps heard her heart saying, "Only yesterday they were little girls, ever so tiny—and now—!" The driving off of a waggonette can be a dreadful thing.

Or the pathos of the scene in *Riceyman Steps* where Elsie goes out to tell Joe that she can't come out with him because Mrs. Arb wants her to stay overtime.

"Look here, Joe," Elsie whispered. "I want you to go home now. But you must call at Smithson's on yer way . . . and get them braces as I'm giving you for a birthday present. I see 'em still in the window this morning. I should have slipped in and bought 'em then, but I was on an errand for Mr. Earlforward, and besides I didn't like to, somehow, without you, and me with my apron on too. But you must buy 'em tonight, so as you can wear 'em tomorrow. I want to say to myself tomorrow morning, 'He's wearing them braces.' I've brought you the money. . . . You promise me, Joe? It's a fair and square promise?"

He made no reply.

"You promise me, darling Joe?" she insisted.

He nodded; he could not speak in his desolation and in his servitude to her. She smiled her lovely thanks for his obedience.

"Now let me see ye start off," she cajoled him. "I know ye. . . ."

They kissed again. Elsie pushed him away, and then stood watching until he had vanished round the corner . . . into the King's Cross Road. She stood watching indeed for some moments after that. She was crying.

Or the tragi-comedy of the wedding and homecoming of Mr. and Mrs. Earlforward, when the day's honeymoon is curtailed because of the wicked temptation to spend sixpences among Mrs. Tussaud's waxworks, and the mutual gifts from bride and groom are a complete vacuum cleaning and a safe, while Elsie, who earns twenty pounds a year, passes like Pippa, buys an old slipper, rice, and a cake, and puts a little warmth into the misers by her own glowing humanity.

Though Arnold Bennett always has a great air of omniscience on the subject of the normal relations of men and women in love and marriage, I think he is, in fact, less successful with that theme than with any other. He will convey flashes of insight into general truths, as when Edwin Clayhanger first awakens to full manhood on finding he has fallen in love with Hilda and discovers that "one of the chief attributes of a man is an immense tenderness"; or he can produce a stabbing sense of reality in individual scenes, like the lovers' quarrel in *The Price of Love* or the breaking of the engagement in *The Roll Call*. But his treatment of the central relationship, though he suggests extraordinarily well its basic quality in human affairs, is nevertheless stereotyped. He seems almost obsessed by what one critic has called the "formidableness" of the female; a wife is simply Woman to him, and though there is variety in his husbands, women, once married, seem all the same. Hilda Lessways, Helen Rathbone, Mrs. Prohack, Lilian, and the heroines of many short stories are all simply The Sex—plausible, dishonest, wheedling, affectionate, unscrupulous, crooked, and clinging!

Indeed, this point might be pressed further into a statement that Bennett always succeeds far better in conveying broad effects or in diffused analyses of developing states of mind than in the direct clash of personality or the moment of intense emotion. A superficial, or what one might call a "constructed," scene of excitement he handles beautifully—scenes such as the routing by Alice in *Buried Alive* of the former Mrs. Henry Leake and her sons, when they come to charge her husband with bigamy; or her evidence in the trial scene of the same story; or an effect like that of the various members of the family gloating over the collapse of Darius Clayhanger. But the moment when Hilda discovers that the man she thinks she has married is a bigamist, or her meeting with him afterwards in the prison, are somehow not very convincing, and while the analysis of the growth of Edwin's feeling for Hilda, and of the various moods he passes through, is most searching dissective work, the later scenes between them in *These Twain* lack the touch of the inevitable.

It is the same bias for amplitude rather than intensity of imagination which makes Bennett so skilful a summarizer of the general in the particular, of universal human problems in individual instances; of the developing manhood of Everyman in Edwin Clayhanger, of the eternal struggle of the generations in Darius and Edwin, of all unwanted spinsterhood in Janet Orgreave and all-overwhelming maternity in Clara. Part of the same gift, too, on a lower plane is his faculty for a pungent summing up of typical things or persons so that they are instantly recognizable. The modern girl, for instance, in Sissie Prohack, when she tells her father that she has decided to leave home and teach dancing.

"I wonder what your mother will say when you ask her."

"I shan't ask her. I shall tell her. Nobody can decide this thing for me. I have to decide it for myself, I've decided it. As for what mother says—that's your affair."

"My affair!" Mr. Prohack exclaimed in real alarm. "What on earth do you mean?"

"Well, . . . you've got to live with her. I haven't got to live with her."

Or the conversational obstinacy of Lady Massulam.

It was not that Lady Massulam was tongue-tied, nor that she was impolite; it was merely that with excellent calmness she did not talk. If anybody handed her a subject, she just dropped it; the floor around her was strewn with subjects.

Or Mr. Cannon's method of making a boarding-house popular.

He always impressed his customers by the statement that he had slept in every room in the house in order to understand personally its qualities and defects, and he could, and did in fact, talk to each boarder about his room, with the intimate geographical knowledge of a native.

Or Mrs. Arb's sensation on going into her bank.

"Somehow they make me feel as if I'd done something wrong, or at least I'd better mind what I was about; and they look at you superior as if you were asking a favour. Oh, very polite! But so condescending."

Another illustration of his genius for broad effects is what is perhaps his greatest achievement in the presentation of life, the brilliance with which he suggests the atmosphere of general environment, of the forces with which the individual is ever, consciously or unconsciously, at grips. He assembles every scrap of evidence which goes to the making of a personality what it is. We see every detail of the time and the place and the human background against which his characters play their parts. We feel the quality of the changing epochs as imperceptibly one age merges into another; we know not only their spirits but the solid details of what people ate and wore and read, what sort of houses they lived in and how these houses were lit, warmed and furnished: how the developing human consciousness was wrought upon by its parents and friends and teachers and work and holiday and traditions, religious, political, and social: what opportunities it had, what it missed, what it bungled. Yet with all the wealth of atmosphere which Arnold Bennett creates about his human figures, they are never lost in it.

He insists not only on the truth that environment influences character, but on the far bigger and more interesting truth that character triumphs over environment. His human figures may be maimed and distorted and stunted and impoverished by their background, but they all have something which is quite independent of it, so that we never think of them as its helpless victims (as we do so often with Wells, for instance). There is something which makes us know that Darius Clayhanger, even if he had not started life as a "self-supporting man of the world" at seven years old, and gone through those awful scenes at the kilns and in the workhouse, would never have had the charity of heart of Mr. Shushions, who rescued him and whom he afterwards forgot. Constance, again, has a quality which reminds one of a piece of Victorian furniture. Her world has made her ugly and stiff and heavy, without elegance or grace or any delicate symmetry of being, yet nothing can mar the innate honesty and solidity which went to her fashioning, the reliability and integrity of her wood.

It needs very little reading in the novels of Arnold Bennett to conclude that he is supremely interested in the practice rather than in the theory of life. The perception of a fact thrills him as the conception of an idea thrills Wells. Both of them illustrate with masterly skill and spirit the unfolding of the epoch preceding their own and that through which they have themselves lived, but they approach that material in

entirely different ways. Bennett illustrates Change
simply as change, infinitely interesting to mark and
analyze in the process of examining man in his environment, but not a matter to theorize about. Wells
sees each step as a possibility in the evolution of
Utopia. Change as change means nothing to him unless it be a stage in development; the present or the
past is only of interest in so far as it may affect the future. Persons, to Wells, are really only of importance
if they can be universalized. We can compare, indeed, the methods of these two writers very well by
seeing them at work on the same theme, in *Marriage*
and *These Twain*. In *Marriage* we are not interested
in the two young people round whom the story is woven
as *individuals*, because Wells himself is not interested
in them as such. It is the question of Social Service
interfered with by Social Hypocrisy, and the problem
of adjusting those two concepts, about which he is impassioned. In *These Twain* our attention is centred in
Edwin and Hilda as two human beings: when they become generalized they do not become universalized into
intellectual ideas, but into emotional and comprehen-
sively human ones, simply into Man and Woman.

Bennett, again, can bring home as vividly as Wells
the horror of poverty and squalor. Think of those descriptions of the district round King's Cross in *Riceyman Steps;* that "dingy, sordid neighbourhood, where
existence was a difficult and dangerous adventure in an
almost frantic quest of food, drink, and shelter." . . .

"A hell of noise and dirt and dust, with the County of London tramcars and motor lorries and heavy horse-drawn vehicles, sweeping north and south in a vast clangour of iron thudding and grating on iron and granite, beneath the bedroom windows of a defenceless populace." Or descriptions like that of Riceyman Square as it lay "frowsily supine in Sunday indolence," of the families in the house where Elsie lodged; of the interior of the meat salesman's room. But he does not use such descriptions for any purpose of propaganda. There is no comment on such conditions: no passionate insistence on their crying injustice to the dignity of man: no appeal to our pity for suffering fellow crea-tures: no insistent determination that such things must cease. Only that quiet and deadly irony which notes that "just opposite Rowton House, home of the de-feated and the futile, who bought a bed for a few cop-pers, the wisdom and enterprise of two railway com-panies had filled a blank wall with a poster, Why not take a Winter Holiday where Sunshine reigns?"

No, Bennett loves to recount detail simply because he loves to mark, with patient acuteness, everything which makes humanity as it is, and which humanity has made as it is. The inside of Mrs. Arb's shop and the inside of Mrs. Arb both arouse his curiosity, and the artist in him longs to communicate that curiosity and its satisfaction to others, with no obscurer aim than to do it as skilfully and energetically and sensi-tively as possible. And how he can make detail live!

Whether it is the light of sunrise on the Thames showing the vast skeletons of incipient vessels through their
webs of staging, or whether it is the way the gas casts
the curved shadow of a dish on a damask tablecloth:
the texture of a woman's apron or the minutiae of a
parlourmaid's work, or the fact that a gas stove so
often has to be extinguished after the first lighting,
and lighted again with a second and different kind of
explosion! Or take a little, absolutely unimportant
scene like that in *The Roll Call* when George Cannon
watches the departure of his children for their afternoon walk.

The parlourmaid . . . amiably helped the nursemaid to
get the perambulator down the steps. The parlourmaid wore
her immutable uniform, and the nursemaid wore her immutable uniform. Various things had to be packed into the perambulator, and then little Lois had to be packed into it. . . .
Nursey's sunshade was undiscoverable, and little Laurencine's little sunshade had to be retrieved from underneath
little Lois in the depths of the perambulator. Nursey's book
had fallen on the steps. Then the tiny but elaborate perambulator of Laurencine's doll had to go down the steps, and
the doll had to be therein ensconced under Laurencine's own
direction, and Laurencine's sunshade had to be opened, and
Laurencine had to prove to the maids that she could hold
the sunshade in one hand and push the doll's perambulator
with the other. Finally the procession of human beings
and vehicles moved, munitioned, provisioned like a caravan
setting forth into the desert, the parlourmaid amiably waving
adieux.

Arnold Bennett's aim has been to render in writing as much of human life as he is capable of rendering, as living and vibrant as that scene of purely external detail. He has done a mass of second-rate work, but I doubt if there is a single novel of his which does not contain scenes which no one but himself could have created so well, and in his finest books, in *The Old Wives' Tale,* in *Clayhanger,* in *Riceyman Steps,* he is a great sustained literary artist. On the one hand a brilliant craftsman, and on the other a man with a width of tolerant sympathy which perhaps has not been met in English fiction since Fielding. "My aim," he says, "has been to keep a friendly attitude: to avoid spleen, heat and, above all, arrogance. I come neither to scoff nor to patronize, but to comprehend."

Joseph Conrad

Joseph Conrad

In the preface to the first American edition of *The Nigger of the Narcissus,* Joseph Conrad tells his readers the story of a preface which he wrote for the original publication of that work.

After writing the last words of that book, . . . I understood that I had done with the sea, and that henceforth I had to be a writer. And almost without laying down the pen, I wrote a preface, trying to express the spirit in which I was entering on the task of my new life.

In that preface, suppressed at the time, Conrad renders the critic the greatest service which any artist can render to one who seeks to understand him. He sets forth, clearly and tersely, his artistic aim.

Art itself may be defined as a single-minded attempt to render the highest kind of justice to the visible universe, by bringing to light the truth, manifold and one, underlying its every aspect. It is an attempt to find in its forms, in its colours, in its light, in its shadows, in the aspects of matter and in the facts of life, what of each is fundamental, what is enduring and essential—their one illuminating and convincing quality—the very truth of their existence.

He appeals by virtue of his humanity to the general humanity of all men:

to our capacity for delight and wonder, to the sense of mystery surrounding our lives: to our sense of pity, and beauty, and pain: to the latent feeling of fellowship with all creation—and to the subtle but invincible conviction of solidarity that knits together the loneliness of innumerable hearts to the solidarity in dreams, in joy, in sorrow, in aspirations, in illusions, in hope, in fear . . .

In short, the artist is a man striving with all the sincerity and imagination that is in him to reveal to his fellow human beings the very truth, as he sees it, of our common human experience, in this common world, in which we all have our common being.

How, then, does Conrad see the world and the substance of its truth? What vision of the reality of the universe has formed itself in his mind and emotions, and forms itself again to our minds and emotions through his art?

"Very few of us have the will, or the capacity, to look consciously under the surface of familiar emotions," he says, and it is true. At any rate, when youth is past, we think all emotions are familiar to us, and we have as much convention in our acceptance of them, in ourselves, and in other people, as we have in the acceptance of our code of manners. We feel things at once familiarly and confusedly, without ever shaping our perceptions into clear outline, without ever dwelling on the complex vibrations which make each human experience a thing apart and unique. It is therefore in his capacity to accept nothing as ordinary, nothing as proved, nothing as unimportant that Conrad strikes the most unobservant of readers. He sees Jim—"a lost youngster, one in a million—an incident as completely devoid of interest as the flooding of an antheap"— and from that flash of negligible time, he builds a tale, perhaps more rich in taste and variety of life than any other book of our generation. Quite apart from all the amazing skill with which the tale is told and its effects accomplished, the whole of the central idea of it expresses the very essence of Conrad's vision of human life. An individual consciousness, floating so securely in the perfect serenity of that night: the test, abrupt, unforeseen: the irreparable, inexorable result: the solitude of that soul as it struggles with its insoluble fate: the gleams of it Marlow gets—"glimpses through rents in the mist in which he moved and had his being": that last view of him, when, as a tiny white figure in the stillness of the coast, he seems to stand "at the heart of a vast enigma": his final passing "under a cloud, inscrutable at heart, forgotten, unforgiven . . .": and the comment,

The last word is not said—probably shall never be said. Are not our lives too short for that full utterance which through all our stammerings is our only and abiding intention. . . . There is never time to say our last word; the last word of our love, of our desire, faith, remorse, submission, revolt.

It is such lives which, near or far, greater or smaller, are the lives of all men, which Conrad makes at least

less stammering and fragmentary for us. He shows
the infinite unimportance and the infinite mystery of
human beings: the unintelligent brutality of existence:
those swooping events which show starkly, in the light
of day, the inner worth of a man, the edge of his temper, and the fibre of his stuff: the knowledge that it is
only "when we try to grapple with another man's intimate need, that we perceive how incomprehensible,
wavering, and misty are the beings that share with us
the sight of the stars and the warmth of the sun." He
shows souls tormenting themselves in invincible ignorance: youth believing that age and wisdom know
remedies against the pain of truth: the whole complicated and acrid savour of existence: the cruel futility of fate: the ironic unfitness of things. Conrad lays
all these bare, ruthlessly, relentlessly: all the earth
with its intolerable load of regrets and tears. He sees
all mankind like the men who sat round the table when
Marlow related the story called *Youth*:

. . . faces marked by toil, by deceptions, by success, by
love; our weary eyes looking still, looking always, looking
anxiously for something out of life, that while it is expected
is already gone—has passed unseen, in a sigh, in a flash—together with the youth, with the strength, with the romance
of illusions.

He sees men eternally deluding themselves, eternally
challenging life, in hopes, in enterprises, in their relations with their fellow human beings, or with them-

selves: eternally entering light-heartedly on the un-
equal struggle, which appears to them at the moment
well-matched. Marlow, "in his eyes that slightly
mocking expression with which he habitually covers
up his sympathetic impulses of mirth and pity,"
watches them, intensely conscious both of their individual vividness, and, cosmically speaking, of the puny
strength of their honesties and their heroisms, their
evil or their despair: seeing the sweep and devastation
of universal forces in the world of man and nature,
and how, whether man plays the part of shuffling cow-
ard or undaunted hero before his fate, he is alike inevitably vanquished, going down to the defeat of death,
leaving the eternal riddle unlightened and unsolved.
And always Conrad sees man alone: perhaps the most
mysterious thing in the whole inexplicable pageant of
existence being that, in a planet swarming with his fellow creatures, teeming with human life, thronged with
hordes and herds of his brothers, man is isolated by
"that indestructible loneliness that surrounds, envelops,
clothes every human soul from the cradle to the grave,
and perhaps beyond." As Marlow says of Jim, so
Conrad, using his favourite image to illustrate his
vision, would say of man: "I don't pretend I understand him. The views he let me have of himself were
like those gleams through the shifting rents in a thick
fog—bits of vivid and vanishing detail." That is the
most that the observer can hope to see—vague glimpses
into those hidden depths where, in almost perpetual

concealment, the soul lives and dies, and weaves the intricate pattern of its fate. No one has written with so profound a sense as Conrad of the terrible exile of each individual soul from those of the rest of mankind: of the indestructible barriers of self: of the vast human enigma which is masked beneath the placid continuity of the everyday world—the bare fact that every being is, in the end, inexplicable and inexpressible, though it spends its existence struggling vainly both to explain and to express itself.

Moreover, though success in his efforts is eternally denied to man, his struggles for fellowship are the law of his being. He cannot escape his humanity. As Marlow listens to the savage orgies described in *Heart of Darkness*, he realizes it.

"No, they were not inhuman. . . . It would come slowly to one. They howled, and leaped, and spun, and made horrid faces; but what thrilled you was just the thought of their humanity—like yours—the thought of your remote kinship with this wild and passionate uproar. . . . And why not? The mind of man is capable of anything because everything is in it, all the past as well as all the future."

In *Victory* there is the spectacle of the Nemesis which inevitably overtakes those who seek consciously to evade humanity, and Axel Heyst with his final bitter cry, "Woe to the man whose heart has not learned while young to hope, to love, and to put its trust in life," while Jim, conscious of the fellowship in him, which has bound him with such close human ties to an entire community, professes himself "almost satisfied" with that. Man, foreordained to failure, yet knows gropingly his ultimate wish, "that subtle but invincible conviction of solidarity that knits together the loneliness of innumerable hearts"; and if, in comment and analysis, it is rather the mystery and solitude of the individual human soul which Conrad emphasizes, in fact and in demonstration it is the continued and ineradicable instinct for fellowship on which the whole of human society rests. There are certain words, not so often expressed as those suggesting solitude and mystery, but more powerful in effect, more solid, which are embedded close and strong, in his art—Fidelity, Loyalty, Honour; in work, in thought, in man's dealings with his fellows and with his own heart—together with the implication that in them, if in anything, the hope of the world abides.

Conrad is often spoken of as a pessimist in his view of life, but it is a criticism which must be made only, I think, by the class of readers one might define as "sloptimists." Conrad might say with Ibsen that it is his business to ask questions, not to answer them; to report, not to prove. His aim is truth. In his sincere and patient pursuit of that aim, he appears to come to the conclusion that life is an implacable and impenetrable force and that to find any ethical meaning in the universe is an impossibility for the truthful observer. But Conrad's care is for life as life, and not as an illustration of, or as a negation of, any moral law. His

interest in life is scientific in its minute and searching
study of human phenomena: it is done for its own sake
or for truth's sake, and readers who want a lesson or
a message from what they read will not enjoy him. Indeed he addresses all such very directly in the preface
I have already referred to, and I cannot do better than
quote his own words:

> [My] answer to those who . . . demand specifically to be
> edified, consoled, amused; who demand to be promptly im-
> proved, or encouraged, or frightened, or shocked, or charmed,
> must run thus:—My task . . . is, by the power of the writ-
> ten word, to make you hear, to make you feel—it is, before
> all, to make you *see*. That—and no more, and it is every-
> thing. If I succeed, you shall find there according to *your*
> deserts: encouragement, consolation, fear, charm—all you
> demand and, perhaps, also that glimpse of truth for which
> you have forgotten to ask.

The question is, therefore, does Conrad make us hear
and feel and above all *see,* as we read his books? To
the general reading public, the idea of Conrad is that
of the great writer about the sea. They think of him
as the author of *Typhoon, The Nigger of the Narcissus,
Youth,* and of other books in which there are marvellous descriptive passages of sea life, sea dangers, sea
scenery, and the mysterious fascination of sailing ships.
That Conrad makes his pictures of the sea live, I suppose no one can deny, but I think undoubtedly the
more one reads of him, the less one thinks of him as a
writer about the sea, and the more one thinks of him

as a great human artist. It is always impossible, with
him, to take the scene from its setting, for his care for
truth insists that the setting of any human situation is
an essential part of that situation; but in all his greatest and most profound moments of drama, it is the human truth which altogether outweighs our sense of
background. And what an amazing range of emotional values he can suggest! He can convey the pure
profundity of Linda's agony at the death of Nostromo
and, with his unswerving instinct for the gesture that
expresses all he wishes to say, show her with her face
set and white like marble in the moonlight "collecting
her strength to throw all her fidelity, her pain, bewil-
derment, and despair into one great cry, "It is I who
loved you, only I!" Or he can suggest the swift, elemental passion of Dain and Nina in *Almayer's Folly*
and the primitive savagery of Almayer's Malay wife,
and the unquestioning trust of Hassim and Immada,
while against the simple clear outlines of such effects,
he can contrast all the stealthy baffling cross-currents
of emotion and misunderstanding which are at work in
Chance or *The Rescue;* all the strangled emotion between Heyst and Lena; the whispering, uncanny mystery of *The Secret Sharer* or the complex confusion
which is at its unceasing ferment in the mind of poor
Jim, as he struggles to give the exact facts.

While his utterance was deliberate, his mind positively
flew round and round the serried circle of facts that had
surged up all about him to cut him off from the rest of his

kind: it was like a creature, that, finding itself imprisoned within an enclosure of high stakes, dashes round and round, distracted in the night, trying to find a weak spot, a crevice, a place to scale, some opening through which it may squeeze itself and escape.

No question here of Conrad's capacity to make us hear, feel, and see, and just as this gift of his shows itself in his creation of scenes, so it works too in his faculty for evoking the whole flavour of a situation in a few words or sentences. The end of the terrible Kurtz, for example, as he lies "with a wide and immense stare embracing, condemning, loathing all the universe" and gasping out, "The horror, the horror," as he dies. Or the stabbing pathos of Jim explaining: "I was so lost, you know. It was the sort of thing one does not expect to happen to one. It was not like a fight, for instance." Or the human truth of Mrs. Travers, "She sat down in a deck chair to think, and found she could only remember," or of Captain Anthony, when Flora in a misery of loneliness and disillusion slammed the door of her cabin and "he felt as if the door had been slammed inside his very breast."

It is perhaps characteristic of Conrad's genius that some of his most powerful effects are gained by indirect methods—by suggestion rather than description, or by an oblique light thrown on the situation from a point outside it. In *The Rescue*, for example, far more of the shattering of Lingard's whole life is conveyed by the report of how he appeared to Carter, than could be accomplished by any direct description. Lingard, above all and everything a sailor, to whom his brig has been his life—who has found her all that Woman can be to Man, "always precious, like old love; always desirable, like a strange woman; always tender, like a mother; always faithful like the favourite daughter of a man's heart"—comes aboard her again after the disastrous events on the island, which have lost him love and honour and left him only life. Carter knows nothing of it all, but, we are told, he

noticed with innocent alarm that Lingard had not looked either at the sky or over the sea, neither at his own ship nor the schooner astern; not along the decks, not aloft, not anywhere. He had looked at nothing!

That is, a man who is sailor in every fibre of his being, comes aboard the ship of his heart and does no single thing that any sailor would do as a matter of instinct. We know at once that it is no wonder that "Carter felt himself more lonely and without support than when he had been left alone." Again, all the finality of Lingard's renunciation and the fulness of his suffering is in the bare, throttled utterance which closes the book.

"The brig is beginning to forge ahead, Sir," Carter said in a warning tone.

Lingard came out of his absorption with a deep tremor of his powerful frame like the shudder of an uprooted tree.

"How was the yacht heading when you lost sight of her?" he asked.

"South as near as possible," answered Carter. "Will you give me a course to steer for the night, Sir?"

Lingard's lips trembled before he spoke, but his voice was calm.

"Steer north," he said.

Conrad is, I think, the only modern writer in English who creates large positive characters of the type of Lingard. Galsworthy, perhaps, in Jolyon Forsyte, but in general, the creations of the moderns exist intellectually rather than vitally: they are apt to spend so much time in self-conscious thinking and feeling, and we know their ideas and opinions so much better than we know themselves. But Conrad's men—Lingard and Captain Anthony, Peyrol and Marlow himself, how robust and strong they are, in head and heart! There is an almost epic quality of feeling about Lingard, that bold and perplexed soul, with that "headlong fierceness of purpose" of his, which invests his obscure design of giving Hassim's kingdom back to him, with the proportions and the passion of a great enterprise. And we have portrait after portrait of those steady reliable men who are the raw material of great reputations, and who spend their lives, unobtrusively, doggedly, doing their duty, and achieving their tasks, irresistibly, by sheer will and purpose. Perhaps it is because Conrad loves best to tell of those lives which are most remote from ordinary social contacts, by reason of race or personality, chance or choice, that men play so much larger a part than women in his novels. Perhaps this is the reason also, that Conrad is not a popular writer among women readers. He is, I suspect, too truthful to appeal to the average feminine mind, which craves a more comforting—perhaps more deluded—view of its own importance in the universe. Conrad might say, with Dr. Johnson, "Love is only one among the passions, and it has no great influence upon the sum of life." It certainly does not, in Conrad's world, and his whole handling of women is done in a very gingerly and timid way, compared with the energetic ease and force of his men. The only full-length figure is Rita in *The Arrow of Gold* and (to her fellow women at least) she is not convincing. We do not believe in her, and the measure of our unbelief can be gauged by a material illustration. We can safely say that no woman—especially if she have a great deal of hair—can possibly coil it up hurriedly and hastily, and fasten it securely and becomingly with *one arrow of gold*. Rita does so more than once in the book and we refuse to believe in her miraculous charm just as we refuse to believe in that lesser miracle. For the rest, his women are pale creatures: mute, like Flora de Barral; hurt, like Mrs. Gould; deserted, like Jim's jewel; misunderstood, like Lena or Mrs. Travers. Always sacrificed, always suffering, as if through some eternal and immutable law. They are not even allowed to have children to compensate them for the pain their hearts are caused by men. To Conrad, the delight of life is the freedom to adventure bravely in any direction a man may want to

adventure, and he sees women as forever and irrevo-
cably barred from sharing in that delight:

This is the pathos of being a woman. A man can struggle
to get a place for himself or perish. But a woman's part is
passive, say what you like, and shuffle the facts of the world
as you may, hinting at lack of energy, of wisdom, of courage. As a matter of fact, almost all women have all that—of
their own kind. But they are not made for attack. Wait
they must. . . . And it's no use talking of opportunities
either. I know that some of them do talk of it. But not the
genuine women . . . they know that the clamour for opportunities for them to become something which they cannot be
is as reasonable as if mankind at large started asking for opportunities of winning immortality in this world, in which
death is the very condition of life.

So that inveterate reporter of his inconclusive experiences, Marlow, sums the matter up, and Marlow is always worth listening to on any topic. What a charm
he has, with his reflective mind and his "habit of pur-
suing general ideas in a peculiar manner between jest
and earnest"; with his quiet irony, his eager inquisitiveness, his gusts of cynicism, his intellectual alertness,
his sure vision, his large human sympathy! It is impossible to say how much the stories of *Chance, Lord
Jim,* and *Youth* owe to the fact that it is under that
alias that they are told.

But Conrad has the same width in his range of masculine portraits as he has in his range of human emotion. He cannot touch a character without making us

feel and see him. From McWhirr with "just enough imagination to carry him through each successive day and no more," to the delicately sensitive Jim, from the thumb-nail sketch of Charley, the ship's boy, who bribes his mother with a drink to stop kissing him in public, to the minutely built up, disagreeable, and despicable figure of de Barral, there is mankind in infinite variety. Dr. Monygham, "whose short, hopeless laugh expressed somehow an immense distrust of mankind": Heyst with his "full and equable contempt" of human life: Donkin with his ceaseless flow of cockney blasphemies: little Fyne and his "senseless pedestrianism." However much or however little we see of them, we know them, familiarly, intimately. We know their hearts, and we know their appearance with all the solid materialism imaginable. We know all about Mr. Jones's gaudy dressing gown, and the tiny silver buttons down the seams of Nostromo's trousers: we see Flora's dress "as plain as an umbrella cover," and little Fyne's golf stockings and Mr. de Barral's collars— and how he walked with small steps and spoke gently in an "inward voice." . . . No, there is no doubt of Conrad's gift for making us see. Think of pictures like that of the Patna before the catastrophe: Schomberg's saloon: or in *Nostromo* things like the club, with its disjointed staircase "guarded by a moss-stained effigy of some saintly bishop, bearing the indignity of a broken nose meekly, with his fine stone hands crossed on his breast": or the procession which brings the silver from the mine to the sea: or a touch like that description of Dr. Monygham in his prison "so motionless that the spiders attached their webs to his matted hair."

To think of Conrad's picture-making inevitably suggests the subject of his craftsmanship in general—of his amazing mastery of the technique of his art. He aims, he says, at appealing to mankind's responsive emotions through the senses, by means of a medium which shall aspire to possess "the plasticity of sculpture, the colour of painting, and the magic suggestiveness of music." Page after page of Conrad's prose might be quoted to illustrate the justice of his audacious claim for the art of language, or to praise the lustre and richness which he has brought to the "old, old words, worn thin, defaced by centuries of careless usage," which are the raw material of his work. As an example, however, of how much colour, outline, melody, and suggestion can be alive in a few apparently simple lines of narrative, let us take that passage where the author of the book receives the package of letters which are to tell the end of Lord Jim.

The light of his shaded reading lamp slept like a sheltered pool, his footfalls made no sound on the carpet, his wandering days were over. No more horizons as boundless as hope, no more twilights within the forests as solemn as temples, in the hot quest of the Ever-undiscovered Country over the hill, across the stream, beyond the wave. . . . No more! No more!—but the unopened packet under the lamp brought back the sounds, the visions, the very savour of the past—a multitude of fading faces, a tumult of low voices, dying away upon the shores of distant seas under a passionate and unconsoling sunshine. He sighed and sat down to read.

It is a triumphant piece of workmanship, but the unique quality of Conrad's writing goes far beyond the mere triumphant use of words. There are readers who find his methods of narrative—particularly his peculiar habit of telling the story at several removes from the main actors in it, and his minute deductive analyses—irritating and unnecessarily complex, but his original blending of his substance and his form is a characteristic reflection of his whole vision of life. He is not concerned simply with a plot, a story, as such. He is concerned to find "the fundamental, the enduring, the essential, the one illuminating and convincing quality—the very truth" of each group of characters and events and emotions with which he deals. The main interest is not what actually happened, but *how* and *why* it happened in exactly that way. Hence all the obliquities and subtleties of vision with which the story is told and through which it comes to the reader have a very definite artistic and human effect. They emphasize continually the suggestion of the complexities which lie under even the most seemingly placid exterior. It is brought home to us continually that an event is not just an event: it is a *different* event to every person it touches. So we get the same situation mirrored for us in many different minds, the same person seen from many divergent points of view. Above all we get the constant analysis of all that may be evoked from the rents in the mist of personality, those momentary glimpses and gleams of reality, on which we must base all we know of human character. Marlow comments on his method when he is patiently building up the figure of de Barral in *Chance*.

"You seem to have studied the man," I observed.

"Studied," repeated Marlow thoughtfully. "No! Not studied. I had no opportunities. . . . But it may be that a glimpse and no more is the proper way of seeing an individuality; . . . If one has a taste for that sort of thing, the merest starting point becomes a coin of vantage, and then by a series of logically deducted verisimilitudes, one arrives at the truth."

Again we come back to Conrad's great central aim— to arrive at the truth. That he succeeds in his artistic quest, to make his readers hear, feel, and above all, see, what he himself hears and feels and sees, there can be no question. For the rest—if, in spite of the brilliance of its creation, that vision is in the main, cruel and uncomforting, the conclusions harsh and hard, we can only say with Dr. Johnson:

"Let us endeavour to see things as they are. Whether to see life as it is will give us much consolation, I know not: but the consolation which is to be derived from Truth, if any there be, is, at least, solid and durable."

A Note on Technique

A Note on Technique

The whole consists in the cookery of the author.
—*Tom Jones*

FORM, style, craftsmanship, technique, or whatever
other word we may find to imply the same thing, is not
a quality tacked on, or spread over or fitted in to an
artist's work, but the quality of the work itself. We
read a novel, and we discuss the vision of life created in
our minds by the author; we criticize the characters
who people the story, its significance in relation to contemporary or universal human and social problems,
its power of evoking sympathy and emotion, its pictorial force, its dramatic vigour, its intellectual fire:
and we forget that the only reason that we are capable
of discussing these questions is that the author has *expressed* them, that is, has used a certain form, style,
craftsmanship, and technique which have conveyed to
the reader whatever ideas or emotions he has experienced. Literature is interpretation of life through the
medium of language: it is language which makes manifest every effect and impression the writer wishes to
arouse and kindle, and the problem of language, of
the use of the medium in all its aspects, is the basic
problem of any work of literature. It involves every-

thing which interprets author to reader; the method of
presenting the action, of embodying character, of suggesting relationships, of painting pictures, of creating
ideas, of awaking the mind or stirring the heart.
Every writer views life and selects from that gigantic
spectacle something which he wishes to communicate
to the reader. The selection he makes shows us the
man; his method of presenting it, the artist; and the
age colours both.

In the salad days of the novel, when the aim of
the story was to pass as much time as possible, and
weariness in the story-teller was the only reason for
stopping, when, moreover, plot and action were the all-
absorbing interest in the tale, the problems of technique
presented little difficulty. Mrs. Pepys was quite happy
wading through the interminable prolixities of sentimental heroic romances, whereas the modern Mrs.
Pepys, though it is evident that she enjoys exactly the
same sort of sentimental selection from the spectacle of
existence, prefers it communicated through the prac-
tised and extremely skilful artifice of Mr. Michael
Arlen. Every age has its own fashion of vision and
hence its own fashion of interpretation, which is modi-
fied and adapted by the personality of each artist. As
we have seen in a previous chapter, human nature remains eternally the same in its emotions and in its re-
actions to emotion: its types are changeless beneath its
superficially changing characteristics, but each age
emphasizes a certain point of view and each great ar-

tist makes a fresh avenue of approach towards general human truth (which is the same thing as saying that he makes a different selection from the spectacle of life). The point can be illustrated from that strange little allegory of Victoria Sackville-West, called *Seducers in Ecuador*. There we are introduced to a group of people each living life under a delusion. A woman believes that she has been seduced by a man in Ecuador; a man that he has a mortal disease; another that he must wear darkened glasses. None of these delusions affects life as a force—that simply goes on; but each alters the *values* of life to the liver, making the world a completely different place, and involving him or her in some especial fate. It is just such a choice or accident which gives the quality to every age and to every artist: life becomes subdued to an attitude and presents itself under an especial aspect; it has a changed hierarchy of values. This has a particular bearing on criticism of the novel, because the element of immediate reality which is, and always must be, one of the most powerful reasons for the popularity of fiction—the fact that the average reader instinctively regards it as a comment on human life as he knows it—makes contemporary dress of very great importance to its effect. Poetry has a universal language which tells of the universal experiences of all time, but prose has not. For example, Fielding's creative vigour is so compelling, his hold on the unchanging essentials of human nature so sure, that his interpretation of life convinces us in spite of the modern reader's rebellion at Sophia's tendency to faint and Mr. Allworthy's to weep, in spite of the stilted vows of the young lovers and the lengthy moralizings of the author. But it is very definitely *in spite of* all this that we enjoy *Tom Jones*, and it does interfere with the direct communication which takes place between author and reader when we can enjoy complete familiarity of language and manners.

To the eyes of the modern it appears as if, in the present day, the bulk of civilized mankind has become increasingly self-conscious and critical towards its general and human environment, and that the main problem of communication has been how to adapt the instrument of language to this enlarged and sharpened vision. The history of the serious novel during the last fifty years is the history of more and more subtle means of presenting the intricacies of human relationships, of accenting the element of the unseen and the unexpressed in the affairs of life.

In the older novels direct narrative, with a running interpretation or comment by the author, and autobiography, were the only methods of telling a story. The first method may be used with greater or with less impersonality, from the continual jogging of the reader's elbow which Thackeray allows himself, to the delicate elusiveness of Jane Austen—but it is all the same method. Both forms are, of course, still constantly used; *The Forsyte Saga* and *The Constant Nymph* are examples of success in the first; Victoria Sackville-West's *Heritage, Tono Bungay,* and *Ethan Frome* of the second (though Mrs. Wharton, like Emily Brontë, finds the difficulty of sustaining the pretence of autobiography, and the machinery creaks a little as the story shifts from the direct to the indirect narrative). By the end of the last century, however, English fiction had come in contact with fresh Continental models which enriched, enlarged, and intensified its scope. Balzac and Flaubert had made it aware of the possibility of presenting character through environment, and Dostoievsky had opened the doors of an entirely new sphere of activity for literary curiosity by shifting his drama from the theatre of general experience to the theatre of the mind. Tchekov, again, had illustrated something of the impulses, desires, instincts, and emotions which can be released into consciousness in an instant of time, and in that discovery was the seed which was to produce the crop of writers of whom Katherine Mansfield is the best known illustration. The artists who feel everything in flashes which sting the nerves and senses, who can convey a whole situation by a gesture—like that of the mother, called to cope with her naughty child, as she stands there "popping her thimble off and on," not knowing what to say or do: who can convey the emotional significance of a whole character in an image, like that of the nurse with a laugh "like a spoon tinkling against a medicine glass": who teach the gospel of disenchantment in sketches from life where existence becomes like a drop of water seen under a microscope, a substance teeming with unsuspected activity, where the reader lives in a tensity of feeling, a keenness of perception and a pitch of sensitiveness—a complete heightened reality—which makes normal life seem nothing but a shapeless blur. The School of Tchekov is only a special instance, but the great majority of the present generation of novelists and their immediate predecessors have made psychology, conscious and deliberate psychology, their engrossing interest, and it is natural that such an interest should entail their finding the older technique too clumsy for their new purposes. As they become more and more aware that the human spirit is all laced about with mysteries, as they struggle to lay hold of what Montaigne calls "the many little nimble motions of the soul," they seek more and more to achieve the subtle and the elusive in the presentation of their material, to suggest the increased subtlety and elusiveness of their selection of material from life. Autobiography, for example, although it is an excellent medium for describing the artist's world, and any action outside himself, fails when we seek a just report of his own nature. If the story is to find its centre of gravity in the life of an individual, that individual cannot give a just report of it himself: he can only describe, as vividly as he can, the things of which he is himself conscious. To know him truly we must be able to watch him when he is unaware that he is "giving himself away"; we must be able to note all the myriad little contacts, experiences, unspoken thoughts, and impressions which mould his actions unconsciously and make him what he is. As the heroine of *Jane, Our Stranger* says, recalling her emotions on the night her husband left her: "One remembers things one has seen and things one did, but not what went on inside one's own impenetrable body and soul, invisibly." It is only an acutely sensitive observer and student of the human heart who can convey the story of such crises. It is noticeable, for example, that all the finest work of the most minute psychologist who has written in English— Henry James—is in the form of indirect narrative. His heroes do not tell their own stories, nor does the author, in his own person, tell their stories: we simply see each character's mind in the making. "We not only share their vision, we watch them absorbing it," says Mr. Lubbock in *The Craft of Fiction*. Instead of the adventures of a story occurring in the world of human action, only, they occur also inside the human being himself: the actors become the impulses and move-ments of the mind and imagination, and we have scene after scene illustrating the dynamics of the spirit, the changes that take place invisibly in a man's attitude to the world he lives in. The author may not describe these changes at all, but the reader can see them actu-ally taking place; can watch experience at its work, and the innumerable gradations of its effect on the ma-turing human soul. Conrad's work provides riches of illustration for the study of such methods, both when the inner drama of his characters is stage-managed subtly by the author, and when it is presented with the additional subtlety of the intervention of Marlow's mind. Or again, a good example of such treatment in a recent novel is that in that very perfect work of art *A Lost Lady*, by Willa Cather, where the impressions of character left on the reader's mind are almost entirely composed by a series of pictures and passages of drama which without any direct analysis by the author create the forces of personality which sway Mrs. Forrester and Niel Herbert—through whose consciousness we see her. Take, for instance, the passage, simple but extraordinarily moving, which tells of his disillusionment; of that moment in a man's life which Housman has sung in *A Shropshire Lad*:

> When I was one and twenty
> I heard a wise man say,
> "Give crowns and pounds and guineas
> But not your heart away:
>
> .   .   .   .
>
> 'Tis paid with sighs a-plenty
> And sold for endless rue."
> And I am two and twenty
> And oh, 'tis true, 'tis true!

Niel Herbert wakes one morning in early summer, when Captain Forrester is away and Mrs. Forrester alone in her house, and has the impulse to go for a walk to the marsh before any one is stirring.

The sky was burning with the soft pink and silver of a cloudless summer dawn. The heavy, bowed grasses splashed him to the knees. All over the marsh, snow-on-the-mountain, globed with dew, made cool sheets of silver, and the swamp milkweed spread its flat, raspberry-coloured clusters. There was an almost religious purity about the fresh morning air, the tender sky, the grass and flowers with the sheen of early dew upon them. There was in all living things something limpid and joyous—like the wet, morning call of the birds, flying up through the unstained atmosphere. Out of the saffron east, a thin, yellow, wine-like sunshine began to gild the fragrant meadows and the glistening tops of the grove. . . .

Under the bluffs that overhung the marsh he came upon thickets of wild roses, with flaming buds, just beginning to open. Where they had opened, their petals were stained with that burning rose-colour which is always gone by noon —a dye made of sunlight and morning and moisture, so intense that it cannot possibly last . . . must fade, like ecstasy. Niel took out his knife and began to cut the stiff stems, crowded with red thorns.

He would make a bouquet for a lovely lady; . . . He would leave them just outside one of the French windows of her bedroom. When she opened her shutters to let in the light, she would find them—and they would perhaps give her a sudden distaste for coarse worldlings like Frank Ellinger.

After tying his flowers with a twist of meadow grass, he went up the hill through the grove and softly round the still house to the north side of Mrs. Forrester's own room, where the door-like green shutters were closed. As he bent to place the flowers on the sill, he heard from within a woman's soft laughter; impatient, indulgent, teasing, eager. Then another laugh, very different, a man's. And it was fat and lazy—ended in something like a yawn.

Niel found himself at the foot of the hill on the wooden bridge, his face hot, his temples beating, his eyes blind with anger. In his hand he still carried the prickly bunch of wild roses. He threw them over the wire fence into a mudhole the cattle had trampled under the bank of the creek.

Story-telling must always depend on a blending of dialogue and description. The novelists of the past and the practisers of the older technique among the moderns are accustomed to use these two forms deliberately and straightforwardly. And so used they still possess their old power. They are capable of interpreting atmosphere as poles apart as the cool and gallant intellectualism of *South Wind*, and the whispered intensity of *The Orissers*, or the exquisite sensuous beauty of *Jennifer Lorn;* of creating a piece of vision in the simple yet perfect outline of *Messer Marco Polo*, or in the more elaborate but no less perfect one of *Nocturne;* of presenting character, complete and firmly drawn, with the utmost economy of words, as in the opening scene of Somerset Maugham's *The Painted Veil*, or that in *The Day of Atonement* by Louis Golding, where Eli confesses his apostasy to his wife. They can give a moment of analysis like that in *The Constant Nymph* when Florence is embraced by Lewis Dodd in the empty church.

In the desert emptiness of her mind, whence thought and sensation has retreated like an ebbing tide, a single bleak idea stood forth, a rock till then submerged and now revealed, for a timeless instant, to the daylight. It was an understanding of his essential hardness, a knowledge that this man who held her so close was indeed no tender lover but a stranger, as cold as ice and harder than stone. Then her true self, her generous love, returning, flooding her soul, bore down upon that frightful image and drowned it in night for ever.

Or a moment of dramatic intensity like that in *Ethan Frome*, when he and Mattie sit alone in the kitchen during his wife Zeena's absence, and Ethan's hand touches Mattie's for a moment.

As they sat thus he heard a sound behind him and turned his head. The cat had jumped from Zeena's chair, and as a result of the sudden movement the empty chair had set up a spectral rocking.

But in spite of the magic which can still be evoked from traditional craftsmanship, it is natural that any living and lively art should seek experiment in new forms. We are never at a dead end of development, as Dr. Johnson, with his usual radiant sanity, and in spite of his devotion to the established in all human affairs, pointed out many years ago.

It ought to be the first endeavour of a writer to distinguish nature from custom, or that which is established because it is right, from that which is right only because it is established: that he may neither violate essential principles by a desire of novelty, nor debar himself from the attainment of beauties within his view by a needless fear of breaking rules which no literary dictator has authority to enact.

Art lives upon variety of attempt and the shifting of standpoints, and whatever its detractors may say of the contemporary world of letters, no one can deny it its energetic and indefatigable curiosity in exploring fresh possibilities in its own kingdom. And like most young things, it starts by pointing out the disabilities of its parents. In a recently published essay on the technique of novel-writing, *Mr. Bennett and Mrs. Brown*, Virginia Woolf throws down a challenge to the "Edwardian" novelists, and declares the arrival of a new age in England, the neo-Georgian. She explains that the same experience inspires novelists in all ages.

Some [Mrs.] Brown, Smith or Jones comes before them, and says in the most seductive and charming way in the world, "Come and catch me if you can." And so, led on by this will o' the wisp, they flounder through volume after volume. . . . Few catch the phantom; most have to be content with a scrap of her dress or a wisp of her hair.

Mrs. Woolf then declares that the Edwardians (Bennett, Wells, and Galsworthy) never look directly at human nature—always at its surroundings; that their one idea has been to interpret character through environment, an idea which necessitates failure, since "novels are in the first place about people and only in the second place about the houses they live in." The Georgians, therefore, have felt that they simply cannot let "Mrs. Brown" be interpreted through environment any more, but that she must be rescued and expressed by some way which makes her more living and more real.

The Georgians, then, on their own showing, are aiming at the same thing as their predecessors—the creation of complete human character. They have no obscure and enigmatical goal which the average reader cannot understand, and they themselves challenge comparison with the older generation in the same field and on the same terms. On equal terms means, of course, that the critic must accustom himself to whatever is unfamiliar in their methods; must be receptive towards a new line of vision, and eager to recognize an extension of his own human and artistic experience through contact with a new human and artistic creation. On these terms, then, let us consider some of Mrs. Brown's new champions and their achievements.

Mr. D. H. Lawrence cannot really be introduced into the discussion, because his recent pursuit of raw vitality in the place of what the normal person means by personality, excludes any attempt at presenting "Mrs. Brown." *Ulysses* too, must be left out of account, simply because it is impossible to criticize that book as a novel to the average reader of novels. If its aim, scope, and method are as profoundly and gigantically intellectual and emotional as its admirers claim, it requires to comprehend it a profundity of intelligence and sensibility which very few of us can hope to possess, and merely to criticize details—such as the complete success of the character of Bloom—must appear to its devotees as much of an impertinence as to praise the dramatic excellence of that old Babylonian creation myth to a Fundamentalist. Of the method of creating character and interpreting life invented by Dorothy Richardson, that method by which we never pass out of the realm of one person's immediate experience, and one person's consciousness is the standard of reference for the whole of existence, I have already said something in a previous chapter. Virginia Woolf herself pushes "the stream of consciousness" method further still. She gives it far more suppleness and dramatic force by not limiting it to a single individual, and her experiments stand at present as the most complete achievements in giving artistic form to the Georgian vision of "Mrs. Brown." In her latest books, *Jacob's Room* and *Mrs. Dalloway,* she illustrates methods of suggesting action and personality, atmosphere and experience which are original in fiction. They are, as is natural, the antithesis of the method by which people are described through a description of the houses they live in. No place that Jacob lives in is ever described: he is built up wholly out of suggestion and implication and fleeting glimpses mirrored in the eyes and remembrance of all who come in contact with him. He lives because he is present in the consciousness of the people who see him in the street, or sit near him in the British Museum, or on the top of a bus: of the charwoman who "does" for his friend, of the don whom he lunches with on Sunday at Cambridge, of the painter he talked to in Paris, of the chambermaid who dusted his room in a Greek hotel. We feel him because he is implicated in the episode of Mrs. Flanders losing her garnet brooch on the hilltop, and of the girl leaving her umbrella in the tea-shop, and trying to read *Tom Jones* and being late for an appointment with her lover. On just such a fine-spun thread of connection and significance is his reality sustained; his portrait stippled in with a thousand subdued touches, in a pose with his full face turned away from the reader. The form and scope of *Mrs. Dalloway* is original and different in yet another mode. It seems to spring from a moment of pregnant vision into the strangeness of life, such as the heroine of Stella Benson's *Pipers and a Dancer* has at a tea party.

Ipsie, looking at her three friends, was conscious all at once of the little occasion as a queer junction of lives. Trailing their innumerable threads behind them, the four faced one another mysteriously. The threads behind them, joining at the tea table, spread outwards in a net over half the world, secret threads into lost lives, lost places and stories, days and delights and disasters. She imagined their four lives like a map of trade routes, their lines converging to a knot.

In Mrs. Woolf's book, the knot is one day, during whose course the fates of several flimsily related characters blend, and are made intelligible to the reader by a very sensitive "feeling backwards" along those secret threads into the past of each. Again, there is no direct statement, but this time it is the pattering drops of all the thoughts and impressions as they shower down on the mind of the various personalities, their spoken and unspoken comments on each other, which construct their outlines. But one must confess that the outlines are a little wavering and misty. Can it be that the houses which people live in do tell us more about them than Mrs. Woolf thinks, tell us something which makes us know, with a sure and satisfying knowledge, the personalities of the Baines sisters and Edwin Clayhanger and Jolyon Forsyte and Babbitt? It is obvious, of course, that the use of environment may be purely artificial and external—as it is, for instance, in Hugh Walpole's *The Old Ladies*—or it may be a mere laborious transcription of the insignificant as it so often is in the work of Theodore Dreiser; but it is the abuse, not the use, of the method which produces failure. It is necessary, of course, constantly to remind ourselves that criticism depends on collaboration between reader and writer. The artist uses his own temperament, experience, and sense of form to achieve the effect he holds in his mind, and whether that effect is conveyed or not conveyed to the reader depends largely on the temperament, experience, and sense of form of that reader. It may, therefore, simply be that we have not so spiritual a sense of life as Mrs. Woolf, and that we cannot apprehend life in any completeness when it is presented to us so immaterially. But the fact remains that we cannot. It is not merely that there is no plot in these novels: we quite agree with Mrs. Woolf that "life is not a series of gig lamps symmetrically arranged; life is a luminous halo, a semi-transparent envelope surrounding us from the beginning of consciousness to the end," but life is nevertheless made manifest to us by the colouring of personality which stains that halo, and that colouring manifests itself to a great extent through externals—through the houses we live in and the clothes we wear and our life day by day with our intimates and with our acquaintance. Surely one of the "essential principles" on which Dr. Johnson insists must be, that human existence is inexorably welded with the surroundings it lives with, and if not actually described, their reality must in some way be unmistakably suggested to the reader, for an impression of the solidity of men and women to appear. Life is not only inner life. Wraithlike humanity inevitably leaves the impression of anaemic humanity. It is noticeable, I think, that the most vivid picture in *Mrs. Dalloway* is that of Miss Kilmer, who is presented unabashed against a firmer background of externals than any other character. The whole of her is there, with her gooseberry-coloured eyes and her mackintosh and all her forty years of ugly, clumsy, shabby spinsterhood: we can feel her in Clarissa's drawing-room, looking at Clarissa's beautiful things, hating Clarissa, feeling cheated, and we can see her in the Army and Navy Stores with Elizabeth, buying a hideous petticoat, eating her tea greedily, or praying self-consciously in Westminster Abbey. But so many of the other figures have, as Mr. Mantilini said of the ladies of fashion, "no demned outline": the writer seems so afraid of suggesting only externals, that they have hardly any externals at all, and we feel rather as if we were trying to construct the plot of a Greek play from nothing but the remarks of the chorus.

This new technique of presenting characters from oblique angles with nothing but the play of glancing lights and shadows upon its half tones, does convey, however, a particular flavour of life on the emotional palate, which is most significant of the present day. It transmits a sense of great intensity to detached moments of experience; it emphasizes the sudden, revealing emotional and intellectual stroke; it probes with searching perception into fugitive and flickering mood, and reminds the reader on every page that as matter is made up of invisible individual electrons, so is experience made up of the silt of unremembered fleeting instants of passing consciousness. It is peculiar in stressing the importance of those individual instants *in themselves* to the almost total neglect of the importance they may have in relation to a general survey of human life—hence the effect of inconsequence which all this kind of writing leaves. Can we interpret this insistence on the "discontinuousness" of experience, as we interpret most of the characteristics, social and literary, of the present-day intelligentsia, by its renunciation of a definite point of view, by its dislike of embodying any activity, cosmic or human, within the bounds of a fixed outline? Is this technique a literary parallel to those painters who attempt to suggest energy by breaking up figures and projecting their parts on to different planes so as to give an impression of movement; who strive to suggest the infinity of design by leaving patterns incomplete; whose ideal is abstract form? The aim of such writers is, presumably, to give an impression of the ceaseless activity of life, while at the same time suggesting the sense of its inconclusive character—its inexorable habit of merely adding day to day instead of building itself into the convenient symmetry of a plot. We are to feel as the heroine of *Streamers Waving* feels: "Circumstances wheel me along like a baby in a perambulator, clutching with ridiculous hands at the lamp posts." This is the emblem of life left by *Jacob's Room* and *Mrs. Dalloway,* and it is accentuated by Mrs. Woolf's repeated emphasis on the irrelevance of the working of the human mind. Over and over again, sometimes with artistic relevance, sometimes surely, without, we find illustrations of how thought will stream from its original source, sweeping the mind far away in the space of a few seconds. An example is the scene of Jacob and Mrs. Wentworth Williams on the Acropolis at night.

Now the agitation of the air uncovered a racing star. Now it was dark. Now one after another lights were extinguished. Now great towns—Paris—Constantinople—London—were black as strewn rocks. Waterways might be distinguished. In England the trees were heavy in leaf. Here perhaps in some southern wood an old man lit dry ferns and the birds were startled. The sheep coughed; one flower bent slightly towards another. The English sky is softer, milkier than the Eastern. Something gentle has passed into it from the grass-rounded hills, something damp. The salt gale blew in at Betty Flanders' bedroom window, and the widow lady, raising herself slightly on her elbow, sighed like one who realizes, but would fain ward off a little longer—oh, a little longer!—the oppression of eternity.

The craftsmanship of these novels embodies to perfection all the sharp, shifting sense of the disconnection, the irrelevance in the facts and experiences of life, in the emotions and thoughts of man's heart and mind, and the uncontrolled impulses of his unconscious being, on which there is so obvious an emphasis to-day. Its interpretation of this vision of existence is elaborate and striking, but with all its brilliance of workmanship, its sensitive use of word and cadence, its feeling for the shapely structure of language, and the exquisite keenness of its human and intellectual comment and criticism, I wonder if it will ever catch a very solid and substantial "Mrs. Brown" in its delicate cobwebs.

Conclusion

Conclusion

"A lady once asked him how he came to define *Pastern* the *knee* of a horse: instead of making an elaborate defence, as she expected, he at once answered, 'Ignorance, Madam, pure ignorance.'"

—*Boswell's Life of Johnson.*

Index

A

Aaron's Rod. See Lawrence, D. H.

Agnosticism of the moderns, 34-37, 136.

Alkestis, 11.

Almayer's Folly. See Conrad.

Anderson, Sherwood, 136, 137, 143, 147-8.

Ann Veronica. See Wells.

Anthony, Joseph.
  The Golden Village, 149.

Antic Hay. See Huxley, A.

Apple of the Eye (The). See Westcott.

Aristotle, 11.

Arlen, Michael, 19, 30, 61, 244.
  The Green Hat, 61-62, 68.

Armstrong, Martin.
  The Goat and Compasses, 64.

Arnold, Matthew, 5.

Arnold Waterlow. See Sinclair, M.

Arrow of Gold (The). See Conrad.

Ashmun, Margaret.
  The Lake, 149.

Augustan Age (The), 28.

Austen, Jane, 5, 20, 32, 107, 109, 116, 246.

B

Babbitt. See Lewis, Sinclair.

Balzac, 78, 143, 247.

Beerbohm, Max, 31, 32, 65.

Benet, Stephen, 148.

Ben Hecht, 139.

Bennett, Arnold, 19, 20, 44, 59, 73, 115, 144, 145, 156, 181, 192, 195, 199-219.
  Buried Alive, 212.
  The Card (Denry the Audacious), 208.
  Clayhanger, 95, 146, 219.
  The Old Wives' Tale, 23, 158, 207, 208, 219.
  Pocket Philosophies, 200-01.
  The Price of Love, 210.
  The Regent (The Old Adam), 208.
  Riceyman Steps, 67, 206, 208, 210, 216, 219.
  The Roll Call, 210, 218.
  These Twain, 212, 216.

Benson, Stella, 38.
  Pipers and a Dancer, 38, 257.
  The Poor Man, 70, 108.

Bentham, Jeremy, 31.

Beresford, J. D., 60, 95.
  Jacob Stahl, 95.

Borden, Mary.
  Jane, Our Stranger, 111, 113, 249.

Boswell, 20.

Brooks, Van Wyck, 180.

Brontë, C., 107.

Brontë, E., 111, 247.

Brothers Karamazov (The). See Dostoievsky.

Bunyan, 58, 178.

Buried Alive. See Bennett.

Burns, R., 15.

Butler, Samuel.
  The Way of All Flesh, 23, 87, 92, 93, 109.
  Erewhon, 78.

Byron, 17.